OPEN UP YOUR LIFE

A Woman's Workshop on Hospitality

Books in this series—

After God's Heart:
    A Woman's Workshop on 1 Samuel
Behold Your God:
    A Woman's Workshop on the Attributes of God
Our Life Together:
    A Woman's Workshop on Fellowship
A Woman's Workshop on the Beatitudes
A Woman's Workshop on Bible Marriages
A Woman's Workshop on David and His Psalms
A Woman's Workshop on Faith
A Woman's Workshop on Forgiveness
A Woman's Workshop on James
A Woman's Workshop on Mastering Motherhood
A Woman's Workshop on Philippians
A Woman's Workshop on Proverbs
A Woman's Workshop on Romans
A Woman's Workshop on Salvation
The Garden of God:
    A Woman's Workshop on Biblical Women
Walking in Wisdom:
    A Woman's Workshop on Ecclesiastes

OPEN UP YOUR LIFE

A Woman's Workshop on Hospitality

With Helps for Leaders

Latayne C. Scott

Lamplighter Books Grand Rapids, Michigan
Zondervan Publishing House

OPEN UP YOUR LIFE: A WOMAN'S WORKSHOP ON HOSPITALITY
Copyright © 1984 by The Zondervan Corporation

Lamplighter Books are published by Zondervan Publishing House,
1415 Lake Drive, S.E., Grand Rapids, Michigan 49506

Library of Congress Cataloging in Publication Data

Scott, Latayne Colvett, 1952–
    Open up your life.

    Bibliography: p.
      1. Hospitality—Religious aspects—Christianity.
  I. Title.
BV4647.H6S36   1984   241'.4   83-21857
ISBN 0-310-38901-1

Edited by Linda Vanderzalm

Printed in the United States of America

84 85 86 87 88 89 90 91 / 11 10 9 8 7 6 5 4 3 2

To Dan —
home is
wherever you are

CONTENTS

ACKNOWLEDGMENTS

Sincerest thanks to four helpful women—Carol Allen, Kathy Stableford, Gail Gallagher, and Helen Champney—who read and commented on the manuscript.

Special thanks to Carol Allen who kept me on the grammar straight-and-narrow.

Sharon Riddle constantly invited my children over to her home which gave me valuable extra hours in which to write. I love you for your selflessness, Sharon.

Diana Story prayed for me and encouraged me constantly.

My beloved husband, Dan, and precious children, Ryan and Celeste, have been unbelievably patient.

Dick Ellis, a fine man from my home congregation of the Pennsylvania Street Church of Christ, actually brought his word processor to my home, set it up, taught me to use it, and patiently answered questions during the two-month loan of the equipment. Greater love hath no man than he turn over his personal computer to a frazzle-headed author with a deadline.

And thank You, Lord Jesus, for Your control over my life and my writings. May they always glorify You.

HOW TO GET THE MOST
OUT OF THIS STUDY

1. Each time you open your Bible, open your heart.
2. Spend some time each day studying the Word and praying.
3. In group study use a Bible version that is both easy for you to understand and technically correct. I suggest the *New International Version* because it uses both accurate and contemporary language. It is the version whose phrasing I have used in study questions.
4. How to use this study guide: This Bible study consists of nine lessons, each of which is divided into two parts—questions for group discussion and "Exploring God's Word Through the Week." The discussion questions are meant to be used as the basis for class discussions whereas the "Exploring God's Word Through the Week" questions are to be used in your home as daily devotional questions which will further explore the theme of each lesson. Although these devotional questions probably won't be discussed in class,

you should keep a small spiral notebook of your responses.

5. Don't come to class "cold." Take a few minutes during the day of class to review the Scripture passage for the week's lesson. As you read, ask yourself why the Scripture was chosen to illustrate the theme of hospitality. Then look over the discussion questions with an open mind so you will be able to understand what others in your study group see in the passage.

6. Choose a prayer partner from among your classmates. Call on her during the week to encourage her in her daily devotional readings, and of course pray daily for her.

7. Be on time; lateness is rude.

8. Make a firm commitment to yourself to stay on the subject in class discussions no matter how tempting it is to share interesting things you know that don't relate directly to the Scripture passage at hand.

9. Be considerate of the doctrinal views of others when they conflict with yours. Who knows, you could be wrong!

10. Always begin class with prayer.

INTRODUCTION

I find I cannot write about hospitality and be hospitable at the same time.

Karen Burton Mains
Open Heart, Open Home

For the past two years I have been living in a state of barely suppressed fervor as I prepared this book. Whenever I have told other Christian women that I am working on a book about our duty and responsibility of hospitality, the response has always been, "A book like that is so needed." But when the actual writing of the book began, I started to get cold feet. I have feared that the publication of this book would cause me to be regarded as an "expert" on hospitality, just as my first book *(The Mormon Mirage)* has caused some people to address me as an expert on Mormonism.

I'm not an expert on anything! My own knowledge of my many failings and weaknesses makes me shrink from holding myself up as an example for others to follow. However, I have shared my home with many people and have seen in my own life and in the lives of my family members what a blessing this has brought to us. I can share my experiences and share what I've learned from God's Word about hospitality.

One warning: If you've decided to read this book just to stimulate your thinking or to give you that "warm feeling" that a devotional book gives, put it down quickly. This study is intended to prod you into action! William C. Martin in *The Layman's Bible Encyclopedia* defined hospitality as "the act of receiving and entertaining guests—either friends or strangers—generously and kindly. The practice of hospitality to a degree that seems strange to us was quite common in Biblical times . . . Jesus' directions to the apostles and to the seventy to take nothing on their journey presupposes that they were to rely upon the hospitality of the people to whom they preached. The conditions which made the hospitality of the Near East a vital aspect of life—chiefly the absence of any other means of sustaining life on a journey of any distance—no longer exists in Western civilization; nevertheless, the precepts given in Scripture concerning hospitality can be easily adapted to the contemporary social situation."

In this concise definition Martin pointed out the essential elements of hospitality:

1. Hospitality is an act which depends for its effectiveness on the spirit in which it is performed.

2. Old Testament hospitality—a tradition of unparalleled generosity to guests—was a welcome way of life up through New Testament times.

3. Bible principles of hospitality, far from being irrelevant to today's church, are desperately needed.

We must begin thinking of hospitality in ways that the world doesn't. The world thinks of hospitality in terms of dinner parties and the "hostess with the mostest." The Christian thinks of it in terms of joyfully and lovingly opening up the door to guests who don't care if you're wearing blue jeans and serving canned spaghetti.

The worldly hostess invites guests in order to enhance the

social standing or sales of herself or her husband. The Christian hostess invites those who need what she can give—nourishment for the body and soul. The worldly hostess frets over the cost of the appetizers she must serve—while the Christian hostess offers her best with no regrets and no apologies.

The worldly hostess entertains. <u>The Christian hostess shares and serves.</u>

It has often been said that a person's home reflects her personality. When we share our homes, we share a part of ourselves. However many churchgoers today would no more share their homes with anyone other than relatives and close friends than they would share their toothbrushes.

We Christians have often made excuses that we're too busy or we're financially strapped or we're too old or we've tried it, but it didn't work or—worst of all—that someone else will do it anyway.

It is impossible to read through the New Testament without seeing that hospitality was not only commanded, it was practiced freely by early Christians. And they loved it! Imagine inviting hungry people to your home, and you have no range or microwave in which to cook dinner, no automatic dishwasher for cleanup!

For those early Christians, hospitality wasn't an option; it was a necessity of life. Neither was it a "gift" given to just a few or even to most. The "gift" that they possessed was both a desire to be around other Christians and a desire to initiate that fellowship.

Perhaps some of the most fertile ground I found in the Bible to illustrate the basics of hospitality was in an unexpected spot—the parables of Jesus. The Great Teacher used those little stories to teach us principles, not just laws, about how to live.

I know that no Bible exegete would claim that Jesus had

hospitality in mind when He told the story about the working of leaven in Luke 13:20--21. But this is a woman's parable—telling about the experiences of a woman in her everyday life. And hospitality, like leaven, can change the whole structure of its surroundings. Like leaven, hospitality works slowly and almost imperceptibly. But look at the results! A little leaven is able to change an uninteresting lump of dough into an active, living mass that nourishes the body. The home that receives guests in Christ's name is changed from a house made of walls and roof into a haven for fellowship and love and spiritual nourishment.

It is our love for Christ which motivates us to hospitality, and through our hospitality we learn to love more deeply. In a marvelous way hospitality and love are bound together in a cycle—love leads us to hospitality which leads us to love which encourages further hospitality.

One of the basic principles of hospitality involves seeing ourselves as a family with God as our Father and the earth as our home. And one of the definite characteristics of families is that they eat together. Christian brothers and sisters have been eating together for two thousand years now. Why, I asked myself, is food so important in the rituals of fellowship?

First of all, food and fellowship are both basic human needs. We all recognize the need for food for proper functioning of the body, but the need for close human relationships is just as vital. Countless medical experiments prove that you can kill children's spirits by lack of communication and love as surely as you can starve their bodies with lack of food.

Another reason why food is an important ritual of fellowship is that food reminds us of our dependence on the providence of God. And it is no coincidence that Jesus told us to remind ourselves of our dependence on Him by the act of eating and drinking. "This do," He said, "in remembrance of Me." He also urged His disciples to eat with Him.

It's no coincidence, either, that the first miracle that Jesus performed (that of turning water into wine) and His last miracle before His ascension (the disciples' miraculous catch of fish) were both associated with a social meal.

The changing of water into wine took place in a home, not in a public place. If you've never experienced a miracle, perhaps you've started your search in the wrong places. When you open your home to others, miraculous things happen in the lives of your guests and your family.

Many times those who haven't yet begun to open their homes to others look at hospitable women and say, "Well, that's easy for them. Hospitality is a natural gift for them." And it's true—hospitality does become more effortless with practice and with the inherent increase in love that it engenders. But in Matthew 25:24, a servant accused his master of the same sort of thing when he said, you harvest "where you have not sown." That same servant, when given monetary "seed" to produce an increase, did just what his short-sighted instincts told him to do—he put his talent into the ground. (Maybe he thought it would sprout.)

"Only one talent?" we might ask. "His master surely didn't trust him much." Did you know that a talent in New Testament times was the equivalent of fifteen years' wages for a servant? Would you say that your boss didn't trust you if he gave you four-hundred thousand dollars to invest for him?

God has given each of us healthy women a valuable talent of hospitality, whether or not we think we can use it. And, like the servant, we will be held accountable if we present to God on Judgment Day our homes with deadbolt locks securely fastened against guests. It won't matter to Him how clean we keep them or how beautifully decorated they are if the sweet fragrance of welcome doesn't waft through their halls. A home without hospitality might as well be buried in mud like the servant's talent.

But I have a great deal of sympathy for the Christian who, upon realizing the necessity for hospitality for the first time, begins to make plans to open her home to someone she doesn't know very well. She realizes that many blessings await her and her guests, but the whole thing seems a little overwhelming! The situation reminds me of a story told in the old McGuffy's Reader, about a clock that stopped in despair when it figured out it had to tick 31,536,000 times a year. But it was soon ticking away again when someone explained that it had to do it only one tick at a time. Anne Ortlund, author of *The Disciplines of the Beautiful Woman,* echoed the same thought when she said, "It's hard by the yard, but a cinch by the inch!"

When I began to write this book, I wasn't looking for radical change in each person who read it. Just a little more hospitality, I decided, would be enough in each person. And then I realized—if only twelve women in each study group would open their homes just once a month to people they wouldn't ordinarily invite—that would be 144 beautiful fellowships in the coming year alone!

And if that won't revolutionize your church and your neighborhood—nothing will!

1

HOSPITALITY AND OBEDIENCE IN THE OLD TESTAMENT

The Rabbis . . . laid it down that there were six great works which brought a man credit in this world and profit in the world to come: study, visiting the sick, *hospitality,* devotion in prayer, education of children in the Law, and thinking the best of other people (Italics mine).

William Barclay
The Daily Study Bible
Matthew, p. 261

God's people in the Old Testament lived under a staggering load of rules and regulations, many of which taught them how to conduct their day-to-day lives. Food regulations were especially important and were strictly observed.

For the most part the Jews did not understand why these rules were given, but they obeyed anyway. Long before trichinosis was identified, for example, the Jews escaped that

Helps for leaders can be found at the back of the book.

disease by obeying God's command to eat no pork. They kept their serving dishes as clean as their sanitation facilities would allow but were spared much food poisoning by not eating milk-meat combinations, just as a wise God had told them.

They were also commanded to be hospitable. There were no Holiday Inns in Palestine, and what few lodging houses were available, were often full (remember the first Christmas?), expensive, and notoriously immoral. Dinner and lodging in a private home often meant the difference between life and death for a weary traveler in that crime-ridden part of the world.

The Jews' mealtimes reflected their lifestyle. They arose early and ate a small breakfast, then went out to do the day's work. Lunch was a light, hurried meal. But dinner was a leisurely social affair, often one to two hours long—a time for family, friends, and guests to relax, talk, and eat together.

The fact that serving as a host—especially to strangers—was taken very seriously is seen in the following two readings.

THE STORY OF ABRAHAM AND HIS GUESTS
Read aloud Genesis 18:1–33.

1. What did Abraham do that indicated he was eager to offer hospitality to "the three men"? _____

_____

_____

2. What did he offer them? _____

_____

_____

3. In preparing the food, how did Abraham show that he was honored to have them as guests? _____

_____

4. After the meal Abraham felt a special closeness to the Lord. What did this special closeness give him the boldness to say? _____

_____

_____

THE STORY OF LOT AND HIS GUESTS
Read aloud Genesis 19:1–16.

5. Contrast the angels' message to Lot with the message given to Abraham. _____

_____

_____

_____

6. Give three clues from Genesis 19 that show that Lot really wanted the angels to stay with him. _____

_____

_____

_____

7. Why do you think that Lot prepared the meal, considering that he had a wife and two daughters? _____

_____

In what ways do you receive pleasure when you personally serve others? _____

_____

_____

8. When the wicked men of Sodom came to Lot's house, what reason did Lot give for his refusal to bring his guests outside? _____

_____

_____

What did he offer instead? _____

_____

How was this "bargain" a reflection of how Lot's morals had been affected by living in Sodom? _____

_____

_____

9. What conclusions could you draw from this incident about the importance to Lot of hospitality? _____

_____

_____

EXPLORING GOD'S WORD
THROUGH THE WEEK

Day 1
Read Judges 19:1–21.

1. Why did the Levite stay so long with his father-in-law?
2. In what ways was the father-in-law hospitable?
3. Look at verse 15. Why do you think the Levite waited in the city square?
4. How did the old man make the Levite feel welcome?
5. Can you think of times when your friends or family—or maybe a traveling missionary—stayed in a motel in your town when they could have stayed in your home? Consider asking them to stay with you the next time they travel through your town.

Day 2
Read Leviticus 23:22.

1. Many people think that the Jews were commanded to share only with other Jews. What does this verse say?
2. In the two passages we considered earlier from Genesis, did Abraham ask the nationality of his guests? Did Lot?
3. What would have been the response if Abraham and Lot had asked the guests what their nationality was?
4. Think about when you might have the opportunity to share your home or a meal with someone of another nationality.

---

*Use these questions as the basis for your daily devotional time. You will find it helpful to record your responses in a spiral notebook.

23

Day 3
Read Romans 12:10–13.
1. With whom are we told to share in verse 13?
2. In what ways could someone be "in need"?
3. In what ways is hospitality a "practice" for you?

Day 4
Read Hebrews 13:2.
1. To whom does this verse say we are to be hospitable?
2. How would you define the word "stranger"?
3. What is a hidden benefit of hospitality mentioned here?
4. When did you last invite strangers into your home?
5. Pray about how you might be able to be hospitable to strangers.

Day 5
Read 1 Peter 4:9.
1. What does this say about the attitude we should have in hospitality?
2. What does verse 8 emphasize?
3. What does verse 10 add?
4. Reread Romans 12:13, Hebrews 13:2, and this passage. Is hospitality optional in Christian life?

Day 6
In the following Scripture verses from the Old Testament, indicate whether the hospitality in each case was motivated by:
     a. obedience to law
     b. love and respect
     c. both obedience and love
     d. not enough evidence to say.
       1. Melchizedek (Genesis 14:18) _____

  2. Laban (Genesis 24:29–33) _____
  3. Jethro (Exodus 18:1–12) _____
  4. Manoah (Judges 13:8–15) _____
  5. Boaz (Ruth 2:14–16) _____
  6. Samuel (1 Samuel 9:15–24) _____
  7. David (2 Samuel 6:12–19) _____
      (2 Samuel 9:1–13) _____
  8. Barzillai (2 Samuel 19:32) _____
 9. Widow (1 Kings 17:7–16) _____
10. Nehemiah (Nehemiah 5:17-19) _____
11. Job (Job 31:16–23; 32) _____

RESPONSE:

Commit yourself to inviting one person or family (someone you don't usually invite) to your home in the next month. If you cannot make that commitment, pinpoint the reason why. Pray this week to have that barrier removed.

2

TWO WHO MINISTERED
TO GREAT MEN OF GOD

What the world lacks most today is men who occupy themselves with the needs of other men. In this unselfish labor a blessing falls on both the helper and the helped.

Albert Schweitzer

Not many of us have the opportunity or even the overwhelming desire to serve God full-time. We may admire someone who labors in the mission field of a foreign land or wish that we had the dedication of our local ministers. But other responsibilities—husbands, children, careers—keep us from fulfilling these desires.

Another factor that hinders us is the realization that full-time work for the Lord carries with it a tremendous load of unique responsibility. It takes a special type of person to carry that load.

---

*Helps for leaders can be found at the back of the book.

If you can't shoulder a load like that, you can help someone else carry it. The Shunammite woman of 2 Kings 4, like many of us, had home responsibilities. However this nameless woman (the only one whom the King James Version characterizes as a "great woman") transformed her home into a tool of service. No, she didn't go out and proclaim the Word—she just helped one who did.

We do know the name of Simon the tanner, who lodged Peter (Acts 9 and 10). But unlike the Shunammite woman's story, his great service is hidden between the lines of the Scripture account. The beauty of the relationship between Simon and Peter is found, as Paul Harvey would say, in "the rest of the story."

THE SHUNAMMITE WOMAN AND ELISHA
Read aloud 2 Kings 4:8–13.

1. How did the Shunammite woman make Elisha's acquaintance? _____

   _____

   What does this tell you about her personality? _____

   _____

   _____

2. How do we know that she had a hospitable disposition?

   _____

   _____

   Contrast how it must have been in those days to have someone in for dinner on short notice with how it is today. _____

   _____

   _____

_____

_____

3. How did the Shunammite woman show a regard for Elisha's privacy? _____

_____

_____

4. What was Elisha's response to her hospitality? _____

_____

_____

_____

Read aloud verses 14–17.
5. How was Gehazi perceptive of the needs of the Shunammite woman? _____

_____

_____

6. What was her first reaction to Elisha's prophecy? _____

_____

How do you think she felt a year later? _____

_____

7. Are all rewards of hospitality immediate? _____

_____

Give an example from your life of a "delayed reward" for hospitality. _____

_____

_____

_____

SIMON THE TANNER AND PETER
Read aloud Acts 9:43–10:23.
Pay particular attention to the mention of Simon the tanner.

8. In today's society is it common for a visiting minister to stay with a single man (such as Simon the tanner apparently was), or is it more common for a minister to stay with a family? _____

   Why? _____

   _____

   _____

9. Look at Numbers 19:11–13. This concept of ceremonial uncleanness was later extended in rabbinical writings to include persons who touched the dead bodies of animals, too. What bearing would this have on the relationship between a person of Jewish background (Peter) and a tanner like Simon? _____

   _____

   _____

   How does Peter's acceptance of Simon's hospitality show an acceptance of Simon himself as a worthwhile human being? _____

   _____

   _____

10. Why do you think that Simon's house was "by the sea"

(Acts 10:6)? _____

_____

_____

11. Where was Peter when he received the vision of the sheet filled with animals? _____

_____

What lesson did Peter learn from this? _____

_____

_____

Do you think God was teaching Peter only about changing dietary laws, or was he trying to convey to Peter something deeper? (See Acts 11:1–18 for confirmation of this.) _____

_____

_____

12. Who were the three men who came to find Peter? ____

_____

Why was it so unusual for him to invite them into the house where he was staying? _____

_____

_____

Day 1
Read Mark 6:7-11.

1. Since Jesus told His disciples to take along no food, luggage, or money, what must He have expected of their hosts?
2. Why do you think the apostles were instructed to stay in only one home in each town?
3. What two actions would cause a disciple to leave town (verse 11)?

Day 2
Read Matthew 10:7-15.

1. What does verse 8 indicate should be our motivation for helping people?
2. How do we know from verse 10 that the disciples went out expecting other people to provide for them?
3. How could the lack of hospitality of a few people affect an entire town?
4. How have your attitudes about hospitality, good or bad, affected someone you know?

Day 3
Read Matthew 10:40-42.

1. To whom are you offering hospitality when you take one of God's servants into your home?
2. What is meant by "receiving a prophet because he is a prophet"?

3. What does verse 42 say to you about how elaborate your hospitality has to be?
4. Are you willing this week to let your minister or church secretary know that you'd like to lodge traveling ministers or missionaries—even on short notice?

Day 4

Paul stayed in the homes of many different types of people. In the following examples, briefly explain the unusual circumstances under which these people offered Paul hospitality.
Acts 9:10–19
Acts 28:1–7

Day 5
Read 3 John verses 5–8.

1. Was hospitality in the early church just for friends and acquaintances?
2. In verses 6 and 8 what were two results of the kindness Gaius showed?
3. What difference between the Christians and the pagans does verse 7 mention?
4. In the area of hospitality, would your actions mark you as a Christian or a pagan?
5. For what would the writer of this epistle have commended you?

Day 6
Read Romans 16.

1. Find here two examples of people who opened their homes to others.
2. In what ways were these people practicing hospitality?
3. If you had lived in Rome then, would you have been on Paul's list of people to commend?

RESPONSE:
Read Luke 22:39 and John 18:1.

The Bible tells us of many instances when people invited Jesus to their homes. However there were other times when a weary Jesus desperately needed a place of solitude like Gethsemane.

Gethsemane, which means "wine press," was probably a private garden located at the foot of the Mount of Olives. It was undoubtedly owned by a wealthy citizen of Jerusalem who, because of restrictions on using fertilizer (dung) inside the Holy City, had his garden on the nearby hill. Such gardens were usually walled and locked, so we must conjecture that this anonymous friend had given Jesus a key. The Lord had been there before (Luke 22:39 tells us that He had gone there "as usual"), and Judas even arranged to have the arrest of Jesus take place in this familiar spot.

What a marvelous privilege someone exercised—to provide a haven for the Lord! You may have a similar opportunity. Ask yourself, "Do I have resources like a motor home, a cabin, or even an extra room in my home that I could offer to a man or woman of God as a 'get-away' place for solitude?"

Pray now for the opportunity to serve by providing for the Lord's servants as Simon and the Shunammite woman did.

3

THE MECHANICS OF FEEDING MULTITUDES

We are perishing for want of wonder, not for want of wonders.

Gilbert Keith Chesterton

Although as an adult, Jesus apparently did not have a home of His own, He nonetheless served as a host on many occasions. From the Scripture's accounts of Christ's feeding of the multitudes, we can learn so much about how the perfect host handled many of the problems that go along with hospitality to large groups.

As the quotation above reminds us, let's not lose sight of the fact that God can do anything necessary to provide for our needs—even our daily need for food.

Helps for leaders can be found at the back of the book.

Read aloud Matthew 14:13–21; Mark 6:30–46; Luke 9:10–17; and John 6:1–15.

1. The miracle of the feeding of the five thousand, as you may have noticed, is told in each of the gospel accounts. (Note: the only other miracle that is recorded in all four Gospels is the resurrection.) Why do you think each of the gospel writers mentioned this miracle? _____

_____

_____

_____

2. In the accounts of Matthew, Mark, and Luke, we are told that a very tragic event had just happened. What was it?

_____

What was Jesus' response when He heard the news?

_____

_____

Do you think He was more saddened by the loss of a friend or by the circumstances that brought this about? _____

_____

_____

_____

3. As news programs on television teach us, some people derive pleasure from watching other people suffer. Do you think this is the reason why so many people followed Jesus when He was grieving? _____

_____

What other reasons might the people have had for seeking Him out at this time? _____

_____

_____

_____

_____

If you had been present at the time of this miracle and had had an urgent need, would you have waited until later to seek out Jesus? _____

_____

_____

4. Look at the accounts in Matthew, Mark, and Luke. What was Jesus' attitude toward the crowd that had intruded on His sorrow? _____

_____

What things did He do for them before He fed them?

_____

_____

5. What was the attitude of the disciples toward the crowd?

_____

What was their "solution" to the problem? _____

_____

_____

Was this a practical and reasonable solution? _____

_____

_____

6. In Twain's book *The Adventures of Tom Sawyer* the title character "painted" a fence by having his friends do it. In

what ways could you say that Jesus originated this philosophy? _____

_____

_____

What details of the story show that Jesus was an able administrator of other people? _____

_____

_____

_____

7. The barley loaves brought by the small boy were about the size of dinner rolls, and the sardine-sized fish were intended to be eaten as a sort of relish on the rolls. It wasn't much, but it was someone's full dinner. If you had been in that crowd, would you have given up your dinner if no one else did? _____

_____

_____

8. When Jesus gave thanks before distributing the food, for what do you think He probably was thanking God? ___

_____

_____

_____

_____

9. Some people say that the disciples passed out small fragments of the food, and everyone was satisfied with just a taste. Examine the Scripture accounts and give evidence for why this could or could not be true. _____

_____

10. Why do you think there was so much left over? _____

_____

If this was a miracle, couldn't God have planned the amount to come out to be exactly enough? _____

_____

What do the "leftovers" tell us about how God supplies people's needs? _____

_____

_____

11. Here are some things that people often worry about when they offer hospitality: size and furnishing of home, cost and amount of food needed, cleanup. How did Jesus handle each of these considerations? _____

_____

_____

12. The John 6 account tells us that Jesus left the crowd after feeding them. Why did He withdraw from them? _____

_____

In John 6:24–25 we learn that the people still searched Jesus out the next day. In verse 26 Jesus identified their motive. What was it? _____

_____

What did Jesus offer to the crowd instead (John 6:32–40)? _____

_____

_____

_____

What was their response? _____

_____

13. When Jesus finished His Galilean ministry, He fed the five thousand. When He finished His brief ministry to the Gentiles in Tyre, Sidon, and Decapolis, He fed four thousand. We read about this second miracle in Matthew 15:29–38 and in Mark 8:1–13. This miracle seems very similar to the feeding of the five thousand. What details, however, would help you conclude that this is a different story? _____

_____

_____

_____

_____

_____

14. At what occasion did Jesus preside as host when He ended His final ministry before His death (Luke 22:1–20)? _____

_____

EXPLORING GOD'S WORD
THROUGH THE WEEK

Day 1
Read Matthew 15:29–38.

1. What was the response of the people who saw the change in those who had been healed? Take time now to praise the Lord for the good things He has done for you in the past day. Then praise Him for good things He has done in the lives of other people you know.
2. Why do you think that Jesus did not rebuke the people for not bringing along enough food?
3. What was His attitude toward them?
4. When the disciples began fretting about where they were going to get enough food to feed the people, they obviously expected Jesus to do something as they had seen Him do with the five thousand. How did He give the responsibility back to them?
5. Examine your life carefully and ask yourself what resources for hospitality you have that you can begin to use.

Day 2
Read Acts 12:20–23.

Here we have an example of a crowd of people who were dependent upon someone for food.

1. Contrast the actions of Herod with the actions of Christ when He was in the same sort of situation.
2. Contrast what each man said.
3. Finally, contrast the sources of power that each man claimed.

4. How do you explain the fact that the Word of God continued to spread in each case?
5. Does this mean that it doesn't matter whether or not we give God the glory?

Day 3

As the accounts of the feeding of the five thousand and the four thousand show, Jesus never allowed a lack of food to prevent Him from trying to make His "guests" comfortable. Doing His best with what He had was something He must have been accustomed to from His earliest childhood.

Read Luke 2:21–24 and Leviticus 12:8.

1. How do we know that Jesus' parents were not well-to-do?
2. A woman I know once remarked that she couldn't provide a meal for the sick, non-Christian parents of one of our young church members. "It's not right for my family to eat beans so I can take food to unbelievers," she said. Do you agree or disagree?
3. Have your children learned from you a willing desire to provide help for the physical needs of others?
4. If they have not, what steps can you take to show them that you are willing to give gladly?

Day 4
Read John 2:1–11.

1. Why do you think that Jesus' mother came to Him when the wine ran out?
2. Mary did not hesitate to take even the ordinary problems to Jesus. What problem in your life or in the lives of your loved ones have you thought might be too "ordinary" for Jesus to help you solve? Bring it to Him now in prayer.
3. Not only did Jesus keep the bride and bridegroom and

their parents from the embarrassment of running out of wine at their wedding feast, but He also gave everyone a tangible sign of His divine nature (note verse 11). What did the amount and quality of the wine He produced show about Him?

Read Ephesians 3:20–21.

4. In a prayer of praise to God, put these two verses into your own words and thank Him.

Day 5
Read Luke 19:1–10.

1. In this unusual story Jesus invited Himself to dine at the house of Zacchaeus. What things in Zacchaeus' life would have caused him to think that inviting Jesus would have been useless?
2. What was the response of the people who heard Jesus say He was going to Zacchaeus' house? How did Zacchaeus feel?
3. Think of a time when you may have felt unworthy of Jesus' presence because of sin in your life. How could Jesus' attitude toward Zacchaeus encourage you?
4. How did Zacchaeus show he intended to change his life after meeting Jesus?
5. How has your life changed since you "received" Jesus?

Day 6
Read Luke 5:27–32.

1. How did Levi (Matthew) show his acceptance of Jesus?
2. How did Levi use this opportunity to share the "good news" with others?
3. Look at the lives of Jacob (Genesis 27:1–29), Esther (Esther 5–7), and Herodias (Mark 6:17–28) to find an example of how each used a meal situation to persuade someone to

do something they might not have done otherwise. What does this tell you about what happens to people's defenses when they eat together?

RESPONSE:

Nicodemus, a Jewish leader who had sought Jesus' counsel (John 3), had an opportunity in John 7:45–52 to defend Jesus against his peers. However the other leaders mocked Nicodemus and silenced him. We hear no more of Nicodemus until after the death of Jesus when Nicodemus provided for a specific "bodily" need of Jesus (John 19:38–42). What was the service Nicodemus provided?

Read Matthew 25:40. Then pray, asking God to reveal to you new opportunities today to provide for "Jesus'" needs.

4

ATTITUDES IN SERVING: MARTHA'S STORY

It's not a matter of impressing everyone with expensive and complicated concoctions, but of your gracious manner and the way you treat your guests. In fact, ostentation and pretentiousness are definitely inappropriate. I am the wife of an Indian immigrant, and I have learned this is an Oriental concept. The best hospitality I ever received was in India at the home of my husband's "untouchable" fifteen-year-old sweeper. They had no chairs, so they borrowed two from an uncle. The mud on the walls and floor of their hut was freshly applied. The children of the sweeper's village took turns fanning me with a deteriorating fan. And what did they serve? One six-ounce, ice-cold Coke that I will remember for the rest of my life. I doubt that anyone will ever be able to top their efforts in showing me how they were honored to honor me.

Linda Mehta
as quoted by Kathleen Fury in
"An Entertaining Story"
Redbook, November 1981, p. 168.

Helps for leaders can be found at the back of the book.

Christian women have noted with interest that many of the secular women's magazines have recently published articles that no longer emphasize the mechanics of "entertaining", such as recipes, party-theme ideas, and ice-breakers. Instead many of these articles have begun to deal with how the attitude of the hostess affects how she offers hospitality.

Linda Mehta's story, which is quoted is a good example of this. This awareness and changed attitude is paralleled in the story of Martha, one of the friends of Jesus. She changed not only her attitude about how to be a good hostess but also her attitude toward someone who seemed to know instinctively how to make guests comfortable and honored.

We see Martha's changed life (which is, after all, what Christianity is all about, right?) in three phases: her first invitation to Jesus, her second plea for help, and finally in her role as a happy servant to her Lord.

PHASE ONE OF MARTHA'S TRANSFORMATION
Read aloud Luke 10:38–42.

1. In this passage, who apparently took the initiative to invite Jesus? _____

   _____

   What does this tell you about her personality? _____

   _____

   _____

   Which other woman whom we have studied had a similar personality? _____

   _____

2. The original Greek in verse 40 says that Martha was "distracted about much serving." What do you think is meant by that? _____

_____

_____

If Martha lived today and were involved in a labor dispute, do you think her complaint would have been, "too heavy a work load" or "unfair distribution of workload among employees"? _____

_____

3. We learn that Mary was sitting at the feet of Jesus. What does this tell you about her attitude toward Jesus? _____

_____

_____

4. Why do you think that Martha took her complaint to Jesus instead of taking Mary aside and privately asking her to help? _____

_____

_____

_____

5. What was the "better," "needed" thing that Mary had chosen? _____

_____

_____

Why could it not be taken from her? _____

_____

_____

6. Was Jesus telling Martha that she should not make any provisions for His physical comfort? _____

_____

What was He saying to her? _____

_____

_____

7. With whom do you identify more in this story, Mary or Martha? _____

_____

Why? _____

_____

_____

_____

MARTHA BEGINS TO LEARN THE MEANING OF LOVING SERVICE
Read aloud John 11:1–16.

8. What do you think motivated the sisters to call on Jesus when Lazarus was ill? _____

_____

_____

Can you give an example from your own life of how you've felt closer to someone after you've had them in your home or you've been in their home? _____

_____

_____

_____

9. How do we know that although Jesus had rebuked Martha on an earlier occasion, He wasn't angry with her? (verse 5). _____

_____

Read aloud verses 17–37.

10. What admirable qualities do you see in Martha that were shown in her first conversation with Jesus after His arrival? _____

_____

_____

_____

_____

11. Contrast Martha's first words to Jesus with Mary's first words when she saw Jesus. _____

_____

_____

_____

12. Why do you think Jesus was so deeply moved at Mary's grief? _____

_____

_____

13. Other than when Jesus wept over Jerusalem (Luke 19:41), we have no other Scripture record of Him weeping, not even when His friend and cousin John the Baptist died. Why do you think Jesus allowed Himself to cry at the death of Lazarus? _____

_____

_____

_____

Read aloud verses 38–45.

14. What characteristics of Martha do we see in this passage?

_____

_____

_____

15. What tone of voice do you imagine Jesus used when He answered Martha's objection? _____

_____

_____

16. What was Jesus' purpose in praying aloud before raising Lazarus? _____

_____

_____

Did He succeed in His goal? _____

_____

17. Who did the "serving" at this meeting of the four friends?

_____

_____

A NEW MARTHA
Read aloud John 12:1–11 and Matthew 26:6–13.
18. Who was honored at this feast? _____

_____

19. At whose home was this feast held? _____

_____

20. What was Martha's role at this feast? _____

_____

21. Who objected when Mary anointed Jesus' feet with the precious ointment? _____

Why? _____

_____

What would be the monetary equivalent today of the ointment? _____

_____

22. Did Martha criticize Mary's actions? _____

_____

What conclusion could we draw about Martha's change in attitude as shown by her apparent approval of Mary's actions? _____

_____

_____

23. If we are to remember Mary for her extravagant love, for what good qualities should we remember Martha? _____

_____

_____

_____

24. What practical advice would you give to someone who was like the "old" Martha? _____

_____

_____

_____

EXPLORING GOD'S WORD
THROUGH THE WEEK

Day 1
Read 1 Timothy 5:3–10.

Think of someone you know who fills these qualifications. Spend time thanking God for this woman, and ask Him to help you to imitate her as she has imitated Christ. Then (as verse 3 suggests) write her a brief note of encouragement or give her a phone call and tell her that you appreciate her for her years of loving service.

Day 2
Read Luke 7:36–50.

Note that this anointing is totally different from the anointing by Mary the sister of Lazarus as recorded in John 12 and Matthew 26.

1. By allowing this woman to minister to Him, what need did Jesus fill for her?
2. What "reward" did Jesus give the woman for what she did? Was this based merely on her actions?
3. In Bible times a standard welcoming ritual included a foot-washing, a kiss, and an anointing of the guest's head. What would be a modern-day equivalent? What did Simon's omission of this say about his inner feelings about Jesus?
4. What did the woman's actions say about her feelings?

Day 3

"I seek you with all my heart; do not let me stray from your commands," said David. "I have hidden your word in my heart that I might not sin against you." Follow David's example today and commit to memory Colossians 3:22–24.

Day 4
A Modern Parable:

Once there was a Christian woman who often opened her home to others, inviting guests several times a month. She prided herself on the fact that she kept her home spotless and that she was a very good organizer of her time. The meals she served were unusual and delicious.

One day, however, she got up to clean her house and prepare the meal for some special guests, but everything seemed to go wrong. Her vacuum cleaner broke, the carton of sour cream she had bought the day before was spoiled, and her kitchen sink clogged up. Then she got a call from the school nurse who said that her son had cut himself and needed stitches.

It wasn't until she was driving home from the hospital that she remembered her guests were coming in half an hour. She stopped at a phone booth to try to call them, but they had already left. So she drove into a fried chicken shop and got enough food for the dinner.

Her guests arrived just moments after she did. To her surprise, they were cheerful and understanding. They seemed to have a special closeness that had never been there before when the two families had been together.

When the guests got ready to leave, the woman guest threw her arms around her hostess. "I guess you've wondered why we have never invited your family to our home. To tell you the truth, everything in your house was always so 'perfect' that I didn't feel I could live up to your standards. Now I know you're human too, and I love you for it!"

1. Compare this parable to what Paul had to say in 2 Corinthians 12:7–10. What similarities do you see?
2. How could the hostess in this story have prevented the barrier that her guests felt in their relationship?
3. Whom may you have intimidated by your strivings to be a "perfect hostess"? How could you start to heal that relationship?

Day 5

There were several women besides Mary and Martha who ministered to Jesus.

Read Luke 8:1–4.

1. Mary Magdalene is the only woman from this passage about whom there is any other information in Scripture. From this passage, what would you say that these women had in common?
2. In what ways do you think they ministered to Jesus? (This passage mentions only one, but what other needs might they have met?)
3. The gospel preacher Richard Rogers said, "The value of work is not determined by what kind of job you are doing or what you are being paid. The value of work is determined by whom you work for." Would Mary Magdalene, Joanna, Susanna, and the other women of Luke 8 have agreed with this statement?
4. For whom do you work?

Day 6
Reread Luke 10:38–42.

Tonight, before you go to bed, make a list of today's activities. Go back down the list and label each activity "loving servant" or "unwilling servant," according to your attitude toward that task today.

RESPONSE:

For the next ten days, keep a record of your activities that involve any kind of service to others. In one column list the activity and in another column record what your attitude was toward that activity. At the end of ten days, evaluate your attitudes. Begin to pray about any attitudes that need changing. Share your evaluation with a prayer partner. Ask her to pray for you and to check with you in a month for any changes.

(Benjamin Franklin used a list similar to this to isolate and deal with his personal weaknesses. "I was surprised to find myself much fuller of faults than I had imagined," he wrote, "but I had the satisfaction of seeing them diminish.")

5

JESUS, THE PERFECT HOST

You give but little when you give of your possessions. It is
when you give of yourself that you truly give.

Kahlil Gibran

If you had the opportunity to spend an hour with any Bible
character, whom would you choose? Would you spend your
hour listening to the sweet songs of the young boy David? Or
would you ask Eve what the forbidden fruit tasted like? Or
how about talking to Sarah, or asking Lazarus what it felt like
to be raised from the dead?

These are tempting possibilities. But none of us after much
thought would give up an opportunity to spend a little time in
the presence of Jesus, our Savior.

How many questions He could answer for us! And what a
privilege it would be to sit at His feet and learn from Him. We

---

Helps for leaders can be found at the back of the book.

could surely learn so much about hospitality from Him, too.

All Christians will have that opportunity to talk face to face to Him. Unfortunately we'll have to wait until after this life to do so. But meanwhile, we have a beautiful Bible story that tells how Jesus hosted His friends. We see in this story how He prepared everything ahead of time but wasn't afraid to enlist the help of His guests. He served food for the body and for the soul. And He left them—and us—with an open invitation to dine at His table, just so we can remember Him.

Read aloud Luke 22:7–13.

1. What was the significance of the Passover feast? _____

_____

_____

_____

_____

_____

2. Why do you think Jesus kept this ritualistic feast when He had only hours left to live? _____

_____

_____

_____

3. Why do you think Jesus had two of His disciples go to prepare the feast instead of doing it Himself? _____

_____

_____

4. Describe the person who was to lead the two disciples to the place where the Passover was to be eaten. Can you think of any other place in the Bible where a man was

described as carrying a water pot? _____

_____

Why was this, therefore, an unmistakable sign for Peter
and John? _____

_____

_____

_____

5. Do you think Jesus had prearranged for the meeting
   place, or do you think the description of the man with the
   water pot was simply an example of foreknowledge? __

   _____

   _____

All adult, male Jews in Jesus' time who lived within
fifteen miles of Jerusalem were required to eat the Passover supper in the city of Jerusalem. Historians estimate
that more than 2,700,000 pilgrims were there the year
Jesus died. Since no one was allowed to charge for the
rental of a room for the feast, accommodations were
probably scarce. Does this information strengthen or
weaken the conclusion you came to in question 4? __

_____

Read aloud Luke 22:14–20.
6. Why did Jesus say that He "eagerly desired" to eat with
   His apostles? _____

   _____

   _____

   In what ways can eating together with people bring them
   closer? _____

_____

_____

_____

7. For what might Jesus have been thanking God when He prayed before partaking of the cup? _____

_____

_____

_____

8. Why do you think He instructed the disciples to divide the fruit of the vine among themselves? _____

_____

_____

What did He say that the cup represented? _____

_____

9. If the bread represented His body, why did He break it Himself instead of letting the disciples do it? _____

_____

_____

_____

Read aloud Luke 22:21–38.
10. We often think that we must only discuss light, insignificant things at mealtime. How did Jesus show that a meal situation is also a time for discussing vital, spiritual matters? _____

_____

_____

_____

11. How did Jesus show by both His words and His actions at this meal the importance of serving others? _____

_____

_____

_____

12. We have learned earlier that Jesus had told His disciples to preach the gospel without regard to their own material needs. Now at the Last Supper He told them to take along not only provisions but also weapons. What do you think He was trying to tell them about what the coming days would hold for them? _____

_____

_____

_____

13. In John's account of the last few hours of Jesus' life, there is no mention of the bread and fruit of the vine offered to the disciples as Jesus' body and blood. However from John 6 we learn that Jesus had already prepared the disciples' minds for this sacrament. What did Jesus say in John 6 about the importance of this? _____

_____

_____

_____

_____

14. As host, Jesus literally offered Himself to His guests. In what ways can we, as hostesses to our guests, offer ourselves to them? _____

_____

_____

_____

_____

_____

EXPLORING GOD'S WORD
THROUGH THE WEEK

Day 1

Scholars tell us that the first *recorded* account of the Lord's Supper is in 1 Corinthians. (The gospel accounts were written later, even though they appear first in our New Testament.)

Read 1 Corinthians 10:16–17.

1. What does this verse say is the result of eating with others at the feast which Christ ordained?

Read 1 Corinthians 11:23–34.

2. What inner attitudes does Paul emphasize here?

Day 2
Read Exodus 12:1–20.

Refresh your memory about the details of the Passover supper; then consider the following:

1. Jesus sent Peter and John to "prepare" the Passover. After reading the Exodus instructions, do you think they did all the actual cooking? Consider these problems:
   - cooking facilities (Can you have an oven on the second floor of a building which had a straw-and-mud-daubed roof?)
   - time factor (Did the two men have time to procure a lamb, have it killed in the temple, and then roast it whole?)
   - ability (Did these fishermen have the know-how necessary to cook a lamb, assemble the bitter herbs

and make the traditional Charoseth—a sauce made of dates, figs, raisins, and vinegar—which represented the mortar of Egyptian bondage?)

2. It's not stretching reason, then, to assume that Peter and John had help with preparing this feast. Can you find in the book of Acts the name of anyone who lived in Jerusalem at the time who might have helped them (Acts 12:12)?

3. Today or tomorrow try to find someone you know who will be having company and offer to supply a dish to help out.

Day 3
Read John 13:1–17

1. What is the setting for this incident?
2. Who was the host in this situation?
3. What essential elements of hospitality did Jesus show His disciples through His example and His teachings in this incident?
4. What did Jesus promise to those who followed His example?

Day 4

1. Customs relating to food were very important to the Jews. Read the following passages and make a generalization about how the Pharisees twisted the original intent of these food customs and tried to use Jesus' actions and attitudes as tools to condemn Him:

    Mark 2:15–16
    Mark 2:18
    Mark 2:23–24
    Mark 7:1–5

2. In a way, you could say that Jesus started a "custom" when He instituted the Lord's Supper. What did He say

should be the purpose of eating and drinking this sacrament?
3. Contrast the way the Pharisees "used" the food customs of their time to how we should "use" the Lord's Supper (see 1 Corinthians 11:23–36).

Day 5
Read Luke 24:13–43.
1. In the story about the appearance of Christ on the road to Emmaus, in what way was Jesus the guest of the two men?
2. In what way did He serve as host?
3. At what moment did Cleopas and his friend recognize Jesus?
4. What proof did Jesus give His disciples that He was not a ghost or a spirit?
5. Why do you think He later ate a piece of broiled fish in their presence?

Day 6
Read John 21:1–14.
1. Imagine that you were an observer standing nearby when the men, weary from a fruitless, all-night fishing trip, were hailed by a stranger on the shore. What was their reaction to the question He asked?
2. How did they act when they discovered that His advice was good?
3. One of the men jumped out of the boat and swam frantically to shore. What did he do when he approached the stranger who was waiting on shore?
4. What did the other men see when they arrived on shore?
5. Who had made the preparations?
6. Who went to get some more fish to cook?
7. How did the fishermen respond to the breakfast invitation?

8. Who did the serving at the meal?
9. How would you describe His attitude toward the others?
10. How did they respond?

RESPONSE:

We often think about the Lord's Supper in terms of the men who attended it. Consider for a moment the role played by some of the women of this time.

We know that Peter had a wife (Mark 1:30, also 1 Corinthians 9:5, where Peter is called by his Aramaic name). Since they lived in Capernaum (Mark 1:21, 29–30), which was about fifty miles from Jerusalem, Peter was not required by law to attend Passover in the Holy City.

Imagine that you are the wife of Peter. How would you feel knowing that your husband would be away on the most important feast day of the year? If you reproached him, what would his response be?

Return now to the present. Can you imagine a time when your own husband might be away on "spiritual business" on an important family holiday? Could you be understanding if you were left alone on Christmas Eve or your birthday or your anniversary?

Or if you are unmarried, think of how you would feel if all your friends were involved in a church project that you were unable to attend. Would you rejoice in their service, or would you feel a little resentful?

This week in your personal prayers ask God to reveal to you ways that you can help to support those who are laboring for the Lord. If you harbor feelings of jealousy or resentment, ask God to heal those feelings and replace them with the attitude of willing service that Jesus had whenever He was helping others either as healer or host.

Finally, commit to memory John 13:12–17.

6

HOSPITALITY IN THE EARLY CHURCH

A teacher affects eternity; he can never tell where his influence stops.

Henry Adams

Oh, to be alive at the time of the apostles! The whole world was buzzing with the exhilarating news that God's own Son had come to earth to live—to die—and then to live again! And though the Son had returned to heaven, He had established a kingdom on earth, and anyone could be His subject!

It's no wonder that those early Christians just couldn't get enough of the Word or of each other's company. We read in Acts 4 that they met every day in the temple courts for instruction, and then they met together in individual homes to eat and to fellowship with "glad and sincere hearts."

Non-believers couldn't help noticing this growing, en-

Helps for leaders can be found at the back of the book.

thusiastic group. The Christians earned the admiration of their neighbors, and daily in the Jerusalem area there were conversions to this wonderful, risen Lord.

The word began to spread—the apostles of this Lord could even heal the sick! And they could preach the Good News in a way that anyone could understand. Soon people from faraway lands began to hear of God's love manifested in His Son. Even priests and hate-filled enemies of these Christians fell under the spell of love. The believers not only surrendered to this Jesus, but many of them gave up possessions and careers to go abroad to tell others what they'd found.

It was in distant Corinth that Paul, a former persecutor of the church, met up with two Jews who opened their home to him. They caught the fire of his enthusiasm, and not only traveled with Paul, but it wasn't long until they were teaching others, too!

What a wonderful time to be alive—then and now!

Read aloud Acts 18:1–4.

1. Why were Priscilla and Aquila in Corinth? _____

_____

_____

What does this tell you about the atmosphere toward Judaic religions at this time? _____

_____

_____

2. What did Paul have in common with this couple? _____

_____

3. How did Priscilla and Aquila show hospitality to Paul?

_____

Were they Christians when they first met Paul? _____

Read aloud Acts 18:18–28.

4. If Priscilla and Aquila were perhaps not Christians when they first met Paul, how do we know that they were converted? _____

_____

_____

5. What additional proof do we have here of the couple's hospitable disposition? _____

_____

_____

6. What did Priscilla and Aquila have in common with the newcomer to Ephesus? _____

_____

_____

7. If Apollos knew only of the baptism of John and the life of Jesus, he must have known the need for repentance and that Jesus was the Messiah. How could his knowledge of the Scriptures have helped him in these two conclusions?

_____

_____

_____

_____

8. How do we see consideration for the feelings of Apollos

in the way that Priscilla and Aquila approached him?

_____

_____

9. Priscilla and Aquila were devoted to Paul and undoubtedly knew of his teachings on the role of women which we read about in 1 Timothy 2:11–12. Do you think that they were in violation of this when Priscilla took part in the teaching of Apollos? _____

_____

Explain your answer. _____

_____

_____

_____

10. How do you think that the home atmosphere created by Priscilla and Aquila must have affected the way that Apollos accepted their teachings? _____

_____

_____

_____

11. In what ways do you think that the couple "explained to him the way of God more adequately"? _____

_____

_____

_____

12. In what two ways did the brethren at Corinth help Apollos in his decision to go to Achaia? _____

_____

13. In what way could you say that the teachings of Paul indirectly had an effect on the people of Achaia? _____

_____

_____

_____

14. What outstanding talent did Apollos possess? _____

_____

How did he use it in helping others to come to Christ?

_____

_____

Read Romans 16:3–5 and 1 Corinthians 16:19.
15. What do these verses tell us about the later activities of Priscilla and Aquila? _____

_____

_____

_____

16. The Scripture mentions the names of this couple six times. How do you account for the fact that in four of the six times, Priscilla's name is mentioned before her husband's? _____

_____

_____

_____

17. List some "reasons" that Priscilla and Aquila could have given for not getting involved with Paul. _____

_____

_____

_____

_____

_____

What qualities do you see in them that helped them to recognize these "reasons" as excuses and to overcome them? _____

_____

_____

_____

EXPLORING GOD'S WORD
THROUGH THE WEEK

Day 1
Read about Gaius in Romans 16:23 and in 3 John; Nympha in Colossians 4:15; and Philemon, Apphia, and Archippus in Philemon verses 1–3.

1. What did these people have in common?
2. Are they well-known characters of the Bible, or do we know of them for basically one good work?
3. Why was the service they provided to the church an essential one?
4. What problems can you think of that might come up in providing this service?
5. Would you be willing to do what these people did on a weekly basis? Why or why not?

Day 2
Read the qualifications for a bishop in 1 Timothy 3:2 and Titus 1:8.

1. Why do you think that hospitality was a requirement for this office in New Testament times?
2. Which of the needs that you listed in question 1 still exist today?
3. These requirements are for men. What qualities do you think a bishop's wife would have to have in order for her husband to fulfill the requirement of hospitality?
4. Do you possess the quality of hospitality to such an extent that your husband is known as a hospitable person?

Read 1 Timothy 5:9–10.
5. Are single women exempted from being hospitable?
6. What relationship does hospitality have to the other "good deeds" listed here?

Day 3
Read Acts 16:13–15.

1. From the information in these verses, would you classify Lydia as basically a homemaker or a career woman?
2. What quality did she show after her baptism?
3. What persuasive question did she ask Paul and the others to convince them to come to her home?
4. What makes you think that she was the kind of person who wouldn't take "no" for an answer?

Day 4

For the next three days you will be considering the effect that the hospitality of the early saints had on the apostle Paul. We have seen the way that Priscilla and Aquila grew as a result of living around Paul.

Although we do not know the names of the disciples in Damascus with whom Paul stayed just after his conversion, we can imagine their misgivings at taking him in. The reaction of Ananias must have been typical.

Read the story in Acts 9:10–19.

1. How do we know that Ananias was willing to obey at all costs?
2. What valid reasons did Ananias give for his unwillingness to meet Saul?
3. How did God answer Ananias? Read Isaiah 55:8–11 for a similar statement from God.
4. How did Ananias address Saul when he first met him?

5. How does this show that Ananias had accepted God's instructions?

Read Acts 9:20-31.

6. How do you know that the other believers accepted Saul?
7. What was the result of this unity (verse 31)?

Day 5
Read Acts 17:1-9.

1. Of what "crime" did the Jews accuse Jason?
2. How did the Jews try to use civil laws to get Paul, Silas, and Jason into trouble? Why didn't they accuse them of teaching false doctrine or of some other religious fault?
3. Can you infer from this story that hospitable people will have peaceful lives and be popular with non-Christians?
4. If not, what other rewards will they receive?

Day 6
Read Acts 28:16-31.

1. Would you describe Paul's legal status as that of a free man? Why or why not?
2. Paul had spent his Christian life living with church members wherever he was. What evidence do you see in this passage that he wanted to "return the favor" to others?
3. In what ways do verses 30 and 31 summarize Paul's life?

RESPONSE:
Read Matthew 22:1-14.

Some of those who refused the hospitality of the king didn't do so because they were too busy committing crimes or doing frivolous things. They were doing a "good job" of taking care of their businesses and their daily affairs. The inescapable inference is that the "business" of God's kingdom—which includes fellowship—is more important than our daily affairs.

Others who refused the first invitation didn't just ignore it like their business-minded neighbors, they were incensed that the king should presume on their time. They even went to the extreme of killing the servants who brought the invitation!

When the king instructed his servants to bring in just anyone they could find, they brought in all kinds of people. What kind of people they were didn't matter—all that mattered was their willingness to come.

Then some of the people came, but they didn't have the consideration for their host to dress up for the occasion. It wasn't the actual clothing that mattered to the king—what upset him was that he'd invited them to the richest feast of their lives, and they had come unprepared, in their grubbies, defying anyone to throw them out.

Isn't that just the way people are about God's invitations? Some are too busy to respond, and others actually persecute His messengers. But this is a picture of the non-christian world. The guests at the banquet are the ones with whom we Christians should be concerned.

We have accepted God's invitation to His kingdom. As a Christian, we are feasting on His goodness every day.

First Timothy 2:9 tells us the appropriate apparel for this wonderful fellowship feast.

Examine your life this last week. Have you been wearing that apparel? What has hindered you?

Spend some time today talking this over with the Lord. Ask Him to help you with the problems you have. And thank Him for the invitation to His kingdom that He offered to you.

7

HOSPITALITY, THE HEALER

Manners are of more importance than laws. Upon them in a great measure, the laws depend. The law touches us but here and there, and now and then. Manners are what vex or soothe, corrupt or purify, exalt or debase, barbarize or refine us, by a constant, steady, uniform, insensible operation, like that of the air we breathe.

Edmund Burke

We think of manners as being those little "extras" that make our relationships with others more pleasant. In actuality, manners are the essentials of any relationship because they are a way of showing that we care about others. In practicing hospitality, the main concern of the hostess should be for the comfort and the well-being of her guests.

The Scriptures are full of examples of people doing "extra" for their guests.

Helps for leaders can be found at the back of the book.

- In Genesis 24 we read of Rebekah drawing enough water for a whole caravan of visitors—welcoming them with willing service.
- In 1 Kings 17 we are amazed at the widow who supplied Elijah with bread before she fed herself and her son in a time of famine—an example of unselfishness.
- In John 13 we see Jesus, the ultimate host, taking the duty of the lowest servant as He made His guests comfortable after a dusty journey by humbly washing their feet.

We can also find many examples in our lives today of considerate care for the needs of others.

- Our friends, Paul and Diana Story, a childless couple, had living in their home not only their nephew (the product of a tragically broken home), but also a battered, young wife and her four children—all at the same time.
- My husband Dan always sets our guests at ease by asking them about themselves—knowing that the most beautiful sound in the world is the sound of one's own voice.
- Helen Davis Pepperdine, the wife of the founder of one of California's greatest universities, often attended juvenile court to see if there were cases involving young girls she could help. She took one such lonely young girl to her own home, scrubbed the girl in her bathtub, persuaded her hairdresser to give her a permanent, and bought her a new outfit of clothes.

What do all these people have in common? They all recognized the fact that hospitality is one of the few ministries where both physical and spiritual needs can be met. They realized the secret of how the home can be transformed into a hospital for healing wounded spirits.

Read aloud Acts 16:16–24.
1. How do we know that the jailer took very seriously the orders he was given? _____

_____

_____

2. What might this tell us about the relationship he had with his superiors? _____

_____

_____

Read verses 25–29.

3. What was a jail of Roman times probably like? _____

_____

_____

_____

What features of a modern jail were not there? _____

_____

_____

_____

4. What did Paul and Silas do to improve their surroundings?

_____

_____

How did the other prisoners react? _____

_____

5. After the earthquake, the jailer wanted to kill himself when he saw all the prisoners freed. What does this show about his commitment to his job? _____

_____

_____

What do you think caused the prisoners to stay in their cells? _____

_____

_____

_____

Read verses 29–34.

6. Why do you think the jailer was trembling? _____

_____

_____

7. Asking two strangers how he could be saved seems an odd thing for a Roman jailer to do. What prior actions of the two prisoners had caused the jailer to think Paul and Silas might have the answer to that question? _____

_____

_____

_____

8. What steps did the jailer take that show us he was truly sorry for the bad treatment Paul and Silas had received?

_____

_____

What physical needs did he fill? _____

_____

_____

9. If we assume that the jailer had a wife, what do you suppose was her reaction at preparing a meal at midnight for two convicts? _____

_____

_____

_____

10. What difference do you think it made that the jailer in-
    vited the men into his home instead of bringing them a
    meal at the jail? _____

    _____

    _____

    What qualities do we see in Paul and Silas that motivated
    them to accept that invitation? _____

    _____

    _____

11. Describe a time in your life that you were able to "heal"
    an ailing relationship by offering or accepting hospitality.

    _____

    _____

    _____

12. How could inviting someone to your home make it easier
    to follow the admonition of Christ for the healing of bro-
    ken relationships found in Matthew 18:15? _____

    _____

    _____

    _____

EXPLORING GOD'S WORD
THROUGH THE WEEK

Day 1
Read 1 Kings 19:1–9.

1. What had happened in the life of Elijah that had caused him to run away in such desperation?
2. What was it about Elijah's "profession" (minister of God) that made him so prone to great depression? Is the same true today, too?
3. What needs did God meet for Elijah?
4. When was Jesus strengthened by a similar amount of time alone?
5. Elijah and Jesus needed time alone to deal with life's problems; how can you be hospitable to your guests and meet their need for solitude?

Day 2
Read Galatians 6:2.

1. What do you think "the law of Christ" might be? (Look at Matthew 22:34–40 for Jesus' own definition.)
2. What is meant by bearing one another's burdens?
3. In what ways can you make your home atmosphere more conducive to helping others bear burdens?
4. If we look closely at the imagery in this verse, we can liken the burden to a backpack. Is there any justification in this verse or elsewhere in Scripture for taking that pack off the back of anyone and opening it up and examining its contents?
5. What definite guidelines can you set for yourself that will

prevent you from prying into the privacy of others when helping them to bear their burdens?

6. What rules can you set for yourself that will prevent you from sharing confidences in the form of gossip?

7. Write down the restrictions you put on yourself in the previous question. Then take them to God in prayer, asking Him both to help you keep those commitments and to make your home a haven for people with burdens.

Day 3
Read Matthew 2:1–12.

The Magi showed us that gifts are a good way to honor someone we go to visit. Simple presents, including food gifts such as a loaf of bread, are always proper, and they make the hostess feel she is being rewarded and recognized for her hard work in preparing to receive her guests.

Think of someone who has offered hospitality to you recently. In the next few days, honor him or her with a simple gift. Be sure to tell him or her that you appreciate the time they spend in sharing their home with others.

Day 4
Read Romans 12:17–21.

1. In what way can hospitality to someone you consider to be your enemy help you to heal your relationship with that person?

2. The "burning coals" you put on your enemies is a way of saying that your actions will provoke them to shame for the way they have acted. How is "killing them with kindness" an effective way to rid yourself of enemies?

3. Think of someone who has wronged either you or a member of your family. Ask God to help you to invite that person into your home, and ask Him to help you find a way to heal your relationship with that person. (He or she

may not fall down and ask for your forgiveness, but at least you'll show you are willing to begin the process of reconciliation.)

Day 5
Read Luke 1:39–56.

1. How do you think the three months Mary and Elizabeth spent together strengthened and prepared them for the miraculous events they would soon experience?
2. What physical sign did Elizabeth's infant give to show his joy at this reunion?
3. Can you think of a time when you went to someone's house just to rejoice with them? Did you feel closer to that person after this?

     Pray now, rejoicing as Mary did for all the good things that God has done for you. List as many things as you can think of—your health, your family, civil freedom, the Bible, your home.
4. Then call up a Christian sister—or better yet, invite her over to your house—and rejoice with her!

Day 6
Read Mark 9:35–37.

1. What important principle was Jesus trying to get across to His disciples here?
2. On a more literal level, what did Jesus say should be our attitude in welcoming children?
3. How do you consciously prepare to make children welcome in your home?

Read Mark 10:13–16.

4. What important and serious subject was Jesus discussing when He was apparently interrupted by the children and their parents?

5. Have you ever been annoyed by your children or those of your guests when they interrupted an "adult" conversation?
6. What lesson can you learn from the way Jesus handled just such an interruption?

Those of us with children at home usually have no trouble making the children of our guests feel welcome and entertained. I have learned much from older women whose children are grown up, though. One friend keeps a floor-level drawer in her hallway filled with plastic bowls, building blocks, coloring books and crayons, scarves and handkerchiefs, odd buttons and empty thread spools, small cars, and other simple toys that appeal to all ages. Small guests in her home are comfortable and rarely present a discipline problem.

RESPONSE:
Read Romans 12:15.

A time of bereavement is a time when hospitality is critically needed, yet most people do not know how to use this gift to help comfort grieving. People of Jesus' time knew this, though, and would even hire professional mourners who brought forth tears by remembering their own dead.

Perhaps the opportunity to use your home to comfort someone who is bereaved may not present itself in the near future for you. But when it does, consider some of the following suggestions:

1. At that unsettled time after a death and before a funeral, remember the needs of the grieving family by taking them food in disposable containers. Consider their increased number of incoming relatives, and offer to come over to their house and vacuum and dust. Take them paper plates and cups, and remember canned soft drinks, coffee, tea,

and other necessities for which they may not feel like shopping.

2. Explain to your children what you are doing and let them help you. Let them see Romans 12:15 in action.

3. Invite the bereaved to your home. Greet them at the door with a warm embrace. Take your clue from them as to whether or not they want to discuss their distress. Don't be afraid to weep with them. Submit yourself as a servant to their needs.

8

EXCUSES, EXCUSES

The Christian may burn out, but he must not rust out.
> William Barclay
> *The Daily Study Bible*
> *Romans,* p. 65

Dr. James Dobson, in his "Focus on the Family" film series, said that the incidence of depression in women is escalating greatly—not because men aren't meeting women's needs, but because *women* are not meeting women's needs. Whereas a generation or two ago, women would meet together for birthing babies or quilting or soapmaking, women today are just "too busy." We have isolated ourselves, and we are paying the price.

We have lots of excuses for not sharing our homes and ourselves with others. Let's examine some of these excuses in the light of God's Word.

Helps for leaders can be found at the back of the book.

Excuse #1: I work, and I'm too tired to have guests in.
Read aloud Matthew 11:28–30.

1. What is the promise Jesus gave here? _____

_____

_____

_____

2. If the burden you are carrying now is not "easy and light," whose burden is it? _____

_____

_____

3. What are some practical suggestions for the working woman who is often tired but wants to be hospitable?

_____

_____

_____

_____

_____

_____

Excuse #2: My husband is not a Christian and won't let me be hospitable because he doesn't like being around my Christian friends.

Read aloud 1 Peter 3:1–6.

1. What is the primary "spiritual responsibility" of the wife of a non-believer? _____

_____

_____

2. Sometimes we think hospitality has to take place during the dinner hour. What are other times of the day when hospitality can be offered? _____

_____

_____

_____

3. Seldom does a non-Christian husband absolutely forbid his wife to invite any of her Christian friends to their home. However, this could conceivably happen. How might "extensions" of the home, such as baked goods, encouraging phone calls, and needlework substitute for "in the home" hospitality? _____

_____

_____

_____

_____

Excuse #3: Our budget is so tight we just can't afford to have people over.

Read aloud 2 Corinthians 9:6-15.

1. The promise in verses 10 and 11 has been called a "circular" promise. How is this so? _____

_____

_____

_____

2. How will your generosity cause people to honor and praise God? _____

_____

_____

_____

3. In what specific ways does this passage say you can be spiritually strengthened by your generosity to guests?

_____

_____

_____

4. How can we be hospitable without spending lots of money? _____

_____

_____

_____

_____

Excuse #4: I love my Christian brothers and sisters, but I am a private person. It's hard for me to carry on a conversation with someone other than a close friend.

Read aloud James 2:14–17.
1. What do you think James would say about loving others but not wanting to have any personal contact with them?

_____

_____

_____

2. Verses 15 and 16 mention specific physical needs. What other kinds of needs do people have? _____

_____

_____

How can you use your home to fill all kinds of needs?

_____

_____

_____

3. What advice would you give a shy sister in the Lord who wants to start sharing her home with others? _____

_____

_____

_____

_____

EXPLORING GOD'S WORD
THROUGH THE WEEK

Day 1
Another excuse: I don't mind sharing my home with my friends, but why should I help someone who has brought trouble on himself or herself?

Read Matthew 18:12–14.

1. Whom did the ones in trouble have to blame for their misfortune?
2. How did love prevent the natural consequences of irresponsible action?
3. Has anyone ever kept you from making a bad decision or "rescued" you from a fix you got yourself into? Take time now to thank God for that person. Then think of someone you know who may be having some problems that he or she caused. Is there a way you can use your home or an extension of it to help that person?

Day 2
Another excuse: I don't have the necessary skills to be a good hostess. I'm a lousy cook, my house gets messy as soon as I clean it up, and I'm afraid people will criticize me.

Read Philippians 4:4–9.

1. How can the gentle spirit of a woman in a home make guests more comfortable?
2. Is God concerned only with our spiritual growth, or does

He care about how we keep our homes? Is there ever a connection?

3. What similarity do you see between what Paul says in verses 8 and 9 and what is said in 1 Thessalonians 4:11–12?

4. One of the best ways to learn to be a good hostess is to model yourself after a good hostess. Think of someone you know who has the "knack" of making her guests comfortable. Call her today and tell her how much you appreciate her service in the Lord. Then tell her the specific problems you are having and ask her how she handles those things. Write down her ideas as she gives them to you, and then take your requests for help to the Lord in prayer, trusting that He will help you.

Day 3
We often limit our hospitality by excuses like the ones we've looked at this week. But the Bible does outline some specific instances in which we are told not to open our homes. Hospitality Hazard #1: The immoral "brother."

Read 1 Corinthians 5:9–13.

1. Why does Paul say it is impossible to avoid contact with sinful, worldly non-Christians?

2. During Jesus' life, did He avoid such contact? What were the results?

3. What do these verses say about offering hospitality or accepting it from people who claim to be Christians but whose behavior shows them to be something else?

4. What relationship do you see between this passage and 1 Corinthians 15:33?

5. What advice would you give a Christian sister who is constantly tempted by her association with an immoral

"brother" or "sister" like those described in 1 Corinthians 5?

Day 4
Hospitality Hazard #2: The freeloader.

Read 2 Thessalonians 3:6–15.

1. What facts from his past convince us that Paul could speak with authority about freeloaders?
2. According to this passage, do ministers of the gospel have the right to be supported by the hospitality of the church without repayment?
3. Do you think this admonition against freeloaders was given mainly to protect overgenerous Christians or to help motivate the lazy? Support your answer.

Day 5
Hospitality Hazard #3: The church-wrecker.

Read Romans 16:17–19.

1. List characteristics of the people this passage warns against.
2. Do you think Paul was referring to church members or to those outside the church?
3. What appetites are served by the destruction of Christian unity?
4. Why is the relaxed atmosphere of a home a good place for the influence of "smooth talk and flattery?"
5. Pray for the gift of discernment that you may recognize those "brothers" and non-Christians whose influence on you makes it necessary for you to avoid social situations with them. Then ask God for the additional gift of being able to show them love without accepting their deeds or their company.

Day 6
Hospitality Hazard #4: The false teacher.

Read 2 John verses 7–11.

1. Give two characteristics of the doctrine of the false teachers described here.
2. What is at stake if we accept false teaching?
3. Why is your home not a good place to teach a bearer of false doctrine?
4. How does having a false teacher in your home make you just as guilty as the false teacher?
5. Do you think this passage forbids all contact with false teachers?

RESPONSE:

It would be simplistic and untruthful to end this section by saying you won't have problems being hospitable. Satan won't let you strengthen yourself and other Christians through fellowship without a fight.

Even Jesus had problems with hospitality. If He ate with sinners, the Pharisees said He was associating with bad company. In fact if He ate at all, someone was always around to accuse him of being a glutton.

Many people I know have the attitude that works don't save us and that, therefore, there's no need to be hospitable since we can go to heaven without it. But we can learn a valuable lesson from Peter's mother-in-law—remember in Matthew 8:14–16 how Jesus cured her of a fever and how she then got up and served Him a meal?

Use your prayer time today to thank the healing God who cured you of the fever of sin. Promise Him that you will serve Him, through your home and otherwise, because He first loved you.

If you are the wife of an uncommitted Christian or a non-Christian who hinders your efforts at hospitality, resolve to submit yourself to first pleasing him as 1 Peter 3 teaches. If you are unmarried, read 1 Corinthians 7:34–35 and spend time today praising God for the freedom you have. If you are the wife of a Christian man who aids you in your hospitality, don't forget to thank a generous God for your mate!

9

THE BEST HOSPITALITY

Anyone can be polite to a king. It takes a gentleman to be polite to a beggar.

Anonymous

Up to this point the focus of this study has been on the practical principles of hospitality—how to invite guests and make them feel comfortable in your home. However there is one type of hospitality that is far superior—and more difficult—than all others. Jesus Himself commended it, and it takes a lot of spiritual preparation and considerable effort. But like anything else, the rewards are commensurate to the cost.

If you have faithfully studied the scriptural examples of hospitality given throughout this book, you will have come to the inescapable conclusion that the admonitions to hospitality were given because there is an urgent need for the fellow-

Helps for leaders can be found at the back of the book.

ship that flourishes only in the home. People throughout the Bible knew what you now know: hospitality is not optional.

This week's Scripture passage is one of the most vividly described parables in all Scripture. You cannot read this passage without deep self-examination. And you might regard it as the "final exam" of this study. Do you pass or fail?

Read aloud Matthew 25:31–33.

1. Look at the parable that precedes this one. What similarities do you see between the parable of the talents and verses 31–33? _____

_____

_____

2. What parables, if any, were told by Jesus after this one?

_____

What does that tell you about its importance? _____

_____

_____

_____

3. What imagery is used in verses 31–33 that mark this as a parable? _____

_____

What information is given that shows us that this is also a story to be taken literally? _____

_____

_____

Read aloud verses 34–36.

4. How do we know that God has been planning good

things to reward His servants for a long time? _____

_____

_____

5. Which of the services mentioned in verses 35 and 36 can be provided through hospitality? _____

_____

_____

_____

_____

Read aloud verses 37–40.

6. What tone of voice do you suppose the righteous used in questioning the King about when they had served Him?

_____

7. What does this tone tell you about the attitude they must have had when they were serving? _____

_____

_____

What was apparently the reward they sought for their service? _____

_____

_____

8. What do you think the King meant by "the least of these brothers of mine"? _____

_____

_____

_____

Read aloud verses 41–43.

9. For whom was hell prepared? _____

_____

What does this tell us about God's plan for humanity?

_____

_____

_____

10. Give instances from Scripture that illustrate when Jesus was indeed treated as verses 42 and 43 describe. _____

_____

_____

_____

_____

Read aloud verses 44–46.

11. What tone of voice do you suppose the unrighteous used in asking the King when they had missed opportunities to serve Him? _____

_____

How did their tone of voice differ from that used by the righteous (verses 37–39)? _____

_____

_____

12. Which group do you think was more surprised to learn that their service (or lack of it) was for the King? _____

_____

_____

13. Suppose that this parable was a "final exam." Why were there no "extra points" given for Bible study, church attendance, or prayer? _____

_____

_____

What relationship do each of these important aspects of the Christian life have with service? _____

_____

_____

_____

_____

14. Are you "sheepish" or "goatish"? _____

_____

15. What is the encouraging promise given in Revelation 3:19–20? _____

_____

_____

How do we know from this that the right relationship with the Lord Jesus is an ongoing hospitality—an opening of the door to welcome a guest and having a meal together? _____

_____

_____

Day 1
Read Matthew 5:13-16.

1. What should be our motive in letting our service be seen by others?

Read Matthew 5:43-47.

2. How could someone who followed the teaching here be assured of being judged a "sheep" when the King returns?

Read Matthew 6:1.

3. Does this contradict Matthew 5:16?

Day 2
Read Isaiah 58:6-12.

1. How is the kind of service mentioned here like fasting?
2. What specific needs are we told to fill?
3. List each promise God makes to the faithful in these verses. Then claim each promise!

Day 3
Read Luke 14:12-14.

1. Whom did Jesus say we should invite to eat with us?
2. What will be our reward for obeying this command? Are there any other rewards for service like this?
3. We read in Luke 14:1 that the host Jesus was addressing was a Pharisee. We know that Pharisees prided themselves on keeping the Law. From what you know of the Isaiah

passage you studied yesterday, was this man a keeper of the law?

4. Carefully read Luke 14:1–Luke 15:2. How does the Pharisees' criticism of Jesus show that His teachings about whom you should invite to a banquet had fallen on hardened hearts?

Day 4

Muretus was a poor, wandering scholar who lived during the Middle Ages. Once, while traveling through Italy, he became ill and was taken to a hospital that served transients. As he lay near death, two doctors came, and after examining him, they stood nearby discussing his case in Latin, the language of the educated people of the day. They remarked that since he was worthless to society, perhaps they could gain some much-needed medical knowledge by using him for some experiments.

When Muretus heard this, he summoned his strength and called out, also in Latin, to the doctors, "Call no man worthless for whom Christ died."

What Muretus was saying in part was that you can't prejudge the worth of anyone.

Read 1 John 3:16–20.

1. What kind of people are we told here to share with?
2. What "reward" do we get from serving such people?

Day 5
Read Matthew 5:38–42.

1. Why is this concept of yielding so hard to obey?
2. What does the world say about people who act as this passage instructs?
3. Think carefully of specific times in your life when someone has asked you for something. In each case, was the

motive of the asker to take advantage of you, or was there a real need?
4. Why do you think that Jesus advised us to give to anyone who asked?
5. What is the alternative?
6. What mistakes might we make if we judged the needs of others solely on the basis of what we could see?

Read James 2:1–4.

1. What dangers are involved in trying to use our own judgment to decide who "deserves" our help?

Day 6
Read James 1:27.

1. This is James' definition of religion. How does it show a concern for both our social and our inner selves?
2. This passage specifically mentions widows and orphans. Why are they an especially good choice for inviting to your home?
3. One good way to decide whom to invite to your home is to decide who really needs fellowship. Here is a list of types of people who are often excluded from Christian fellowship. Beside each listing, write the name of someone you know who fits in that category.

Widow _____

Widower _____

Orphan _____

Divorced person _____

Elderly man or woman _____

Person without a car or who lives far
from your neighborhood _____

Person who has recently lost
a loved one in death _____

Family with retarded child _____

Christian with a non-Christian mate _____

College student away from home _____

Military person away from home _____

Person whose spouse is
on a business trip _____

Unmarried adult _____

Person who just moved
into your community _____

Person with a terminal illness _____

Person having financial difficulty _____

Person who has a
loved one in the hospital _____

Those who have been Christians for less than one year (a
critical time) _____

Person who has confessed sin and is
trying to change his or her life _____

Non-Christian who
is searching for truth _____

Family with lots of children _____

Person with physical handicaps _____

International exchange student _____

Battered woman _____

Abused child _____

This is obviously an incomplete list. You will undoubtedly think of others. But the only prerequisite for the list is this: the person on the list must need your help as much or more than you need them.

RESPONSE:

There will be many barriers that Satan will put in your way as you strive to develop your talent of hospitality. Some of them will fall under the headings of "excuses" that were listed in Chapter 8.

But one of the biggest hindrances you will have is your best friend.

"What? My best friend?" you may say. "But my best friend is a Christian! She helps me so much spiritually! I just love being around her!"

Of course you love being around her. That's why she is your best friend. And if she's a Christian, she loves you unselfishly.

Unfortunately sometimes we fall into a rut with people whose company we enjoy. We invite them over all the time and think of them first whenever we think of hospitality.

This week, call up your best friend. Tell her of what you've learned about "the best hospitality"—that which is offered to people who really need it. Tell her that for one week each month you are going to "fast" from enjoying her company. You will call her and keep in touch, but you are offering up that week of the month to the Lord, to open your home to others.

Then look back over the list that you made yesterday and begin to enjoy the true riches of offering hospitality.

May God richly bless you!

HELPS FOR LEADERS

1 / HOSPITALITY AND OBEDIENCE IN THE OLD TESTAMENT

The Story of Abraham and His Guests

Q1. Abraham hurried to meet the "men," showed respect by bowing to them, and begged them to stay.

One point that will undoubtedly come up in this discussion is the identity of the three men. The passage mentions three people, but Abraham communicates mainly with just one. The *Zondervan Pictorial Encyclopedia of the Bible* says: "Their leader is clearly identified with the Lord, whereas the other two are merely angels. There are no grounds for questioning the very early and traditional Christian interpretation that in these cases there is a preincarnation manifestation of the second person of the Trinity, whether He is called 'the Lord' or 'the Angel of the Lord.'" This is borne out in the fact that Abraham said that he had spoken to the Lord (Verse 31).

Q2. He offered them water to wash their feet, an opportunity to rest, and a meal.

Q3. He didn't give them leftovers; under his supervision Abraham saw that everything was freshly prepared from only the finest ingredients. He also showed respect for them by allowing them to eat while he stood nearby.

Q4. As we will see over and over in other Bible accounts, there is something about offering hospitality that brings about a special closeness between host and guest. This new rapport allowed Abraham to do what few men have had the courage to do—to bargain with the Lord.

The Story of Lot and His Guests

Q5. Whereas the angels had brought good news to Abraham—the promise of a son—they had no such glad message for Lot. It is interesting to note that Lot didn't attempt to talk the messengers out of the coming destruction as Abraham had, in spite of the fact that it was his home that was in peril.

Q6. Lot got up to meet them, bowed down to them, and overcame their objections to his hospitality by insisting that they come. He probably knew that if they spent the night in the square, as they had intended, their lives would be endangered.

Q7. It could be that Lot just wanted to have the pleasure of serving them himself. But, from what we learn of his wife and daughters later in this chapter, they were neither particularly obedient nor responsible.

Q8. Lot cited the fact that the men had come under the protection of his roof which shows us that hospitality was at this time a very sacred responsibility. He offered his daughters instead. We are shocked by this, but it may be explained by the fact that Lot may have anticipated that the men would refuse this compromise because they were so determined to have sexual relations with the two angels. However the sexual abandon and worldliness we see in the later conduct of his daughters might indicate that the girls themselves were willing. We see in Lot the result of trying to live among totally degenerate people. It is sad that the Lord Himself did not come to visit Lot as He had Abraham. And Lot must not have been a very good example to his sons-in-law because they thought he was joking about the coming destruction of the city. Lot himself must not have fully believed, because the angels had to physically pull him along with his wife and daughters out of the city when Lot hesitated.

Q9. No matter what we may think of Lot, we know that God loved him enough to save him out of Sodom. We should remember Lot as an example of the fact that in the Old Testament, a host was totally responsible for the comfort and safety of his guests.

At the end of this lesson, the discussion leader should set aside ten minutes to discuss the sections of each chapter that are entitled, "Exploring God's Word Through the Week." Explain that these are intended to be used as the basis of each class member's private daily devotionals and will amplify the theme of each lesson discussed in the weekly chapters by showing other scriptural examples.

Encourage each class member to select a prayer partner from among her classmates with whom she can discuss the daily readings. Also, keeping a small spiral notebook for answers to the "Exploring God's Word Through the Week" questions will be very helpful.

2 / TWO WHO MINISTERED TO GREAT MEN OF GOD

The Shunammite Woman and Elisha

Q1. We are drawn to the Shunammite woman because she seems so modern—she apparently met Elisha by accident, recognized in him a true servant of God, and urged him to come to her home for a meal. She seems like the sort of woman who simply would not take "no" for an answer.

Q2. Elisha must have felt welcome and comfortable in the home of the Shunammite woman because he always ate at her home. Since he couldn't phone ahead to tell her he was coming, she must have either constantly prepared extra food just in case he might come (and remember you couldn't refrigerate leftovers in those days), or she must have been willing to be "surprised" and prepare meals on short notice. Often preparing a meal in those days meant catching, killing, skinning, bleeding, and cutting up the meat entree before you began to cook it. If you wanted extra milk, you would have to catch the cow or goat and milk it. Vegetables, such as lentils, cucumbers, squash, peas, lettuce, and onions wouldn't keep well in the heat of the day, so they were either left on the vine or bought fresh at the city market in the morning. Preparing extra bread often meant grinding the meal, making a fire, and constantly watching the baking process. Obviously the Shunammite woman's open invitation to Elisha shows her to be a very loving, industrious, unselfish person.

Q3. We see here another quality of this woman—she was someone who planned ahead for the comfort of her guests. She must also have had a good relationship with her husband, who apparently agreed with her idea of making a small, private room on their roof where Elisha could have some time alone. She probably realized that God's full-time workers have great rewards for their service, but they usually don't have a lot of time for the prayer, study, and meditation that men and women of God (and we!) need. Often ministers must give up much-needed sleep or recreational time because of their dedication to prayer and study.

Q4. Elisha obviously enjoyed the considerate atmosphere of the Shunammite woman's home. He recognized that she had gone to a great deal of trouble for his sake (verse 13). He wasn't afraid to use what was an apparently considerable amount of political clout to help her (verses 14–17).

Q5. Elisha's servant, Gehazi, must have known that the Shunammite woman's generous spirit would be thrilled with a more permanent "guest" in her home—her own child. Barren women of Bible times were often looked down upon by those who had children, so Gehazi was suggesting a social reprieve for this lady. It is a credit to her buoyant personality that she had not persisted in self-pity for her childless condition but that she had found other ways to serve.

Q6. The Shunammite woman must have given up active hope for a child since her husband was so old. She could hardly believe her ears, but she also didn't want to be teased. However, Elisha's prophecy came true, and she must have been filled with great joy. She was undoubtedly a great witness in her community of how God rewards those who serve His ministers.

Q7. Leaders should encourage all class members to contribute an example from their lives or from the lives of others. Be sensitive, though, to the feelings of those who may not be able to think of an example or who feel too shy to contribute.

Simon the Tanner and Peter

Q8. Possible responses to this situation:
The lax morals of our time make people suspicious of men who live together.

Many men who live alone do not consider themselves to be good hosts because they sometimes do not cook much or keep their homes tidy. Also many single men have filled their schedules with career activities and recreation and do not spend much time in their homes.

Singles in our society are not offered hospitality by others very often, and they sometimes feel awkward offering it themselves.

A single man might reason that a minister who has left his family behind to go on a trip might prefer being around a family.

Q9. We're told that Simon's profession was tanning leather. (Background: leather tanning is a time-consuming process. The basic procedure hasn't changed much since Bible times. An animal must be skinned soon after it is slaughtered. The skin is covered with salt to keep it from decomposing. It is soaked and rinsed repeatedly, then scraped, and later put into large vats of chemicals. It was an art that was passed from father to son.)

Peter had to make a special effort to show love by accepting Simon's hospitality. For one thing, Simon was by virtue of his profession always ceremonially unclean. And if you've ever been around a tannery or persons who have been involved in the tanning process, you know there is a very unpleasant odor associated with them.

Under rabbinical law a woman could not divorce her husband under any circumstances. However she could force him to divorce her if he had a loathsome disease (like leprosy), if he threatened to take her away from her homeland, or if he were a tanner. This shows us just how undesirable this tanner must have been. And it leads us to the conclusion that perhaps the omission of Simon's wife's name was not accidental—it is probable that he didn't have a wife.

Q10. Large amounts of water are necessary in the tanning process. Also the stench associated with Simon's profession probably required him to live away from other people.

Q11. God chose to honor Simon's hospitality by immortalizing his home as the site of one of the most memorable visions given in all Scripture. From this vision Peter learned not only that all of God's creatures were released from the dietary restrictions of the Old Law, but also that all persons—even Gentiles—could receive the good news.

Q12. Peter was still trying to sort out the meanings of his vision when three Gentiles came to the door. Normally a strict Jew would not have dreamed of asking Gentiles to come into the house where he was staying, but Peter had been prepared for their coming and was hospitable to them. This is a wonderful example of how accepting people as they are causes racial and class barriers to disappear.

3 / THE MECHANICS OF FEEDING MULTITUDES

Q1. Probably the large number of witnesses to this miracle caused each gospel writer to record it. The miracle also showed how Jesus was concerned with the physical as well as the spiritual needs of His followers.

Q2. When Jesus heard about the death of his cousin John, He wanted to be alone for a while with His disciples. The class leader should encourage class members who have not yet participated in discussion to offer their opinions on the last part of this question.

Q3. Possible reasons people followed Jesus:
    a. Some people may have been curious.

b. Some may have wanted to try to get Him to stumble in some way during this trying time.

c. Others may have had a sincere desire to try to comfort Him.

d. Others may have had an urgent need for healing or guidance.

Q4. Luke says that Jesus welcomed the people. He filled their emotional needs by having compassion on them, their spiritual needs by teaching them about the Kingdom of God, and their physical needs by healing their sick—all before He fed them.

Q5. The apostles were obviously annoyed at the crowds and perhaps even a little jealous. They wanted to get rid of the hangers-on as soon as possible. At the time it probably seemed like a reasonable idea because, as they pointed out, they were in a remote area where there were no facilities for food and lodging. Sometimes, though, God overrules our "practical," self-centered solutions to our problems by pouring out His measureless love as He did here.

Q6. One quality of a great leader is that he or she efficiently delegates responsibilities to others. In this case, Jesus first turned over responsibility to His disciples by telling them, "you give them something to eat." Then He gave His disciples the job of dividing up the people so that the food distribution could proceed in an orderly manner. Finally He let His disciples share in the joy of service by letting them pass out the food. Someone else who was concerned with "showing off" would not have let his followers have the active part that Jesus did.

Q7. Encourage a response from each class member.

Q8. It seems Jesus was thanking His Father not only for the food but also quite possibly for the generosity of the small boy, the trust and obedience of the crowd, and the great opportunity to show them God's providence.

Q9. The great amount of food left over would invalidate this theory.

Q10. The leftovers were incontrovertible proof that a miracle had occurred. The leftovers were also a way of showing that God doesn't just give us the necessities; He fills our cups to overflowing—and then keeps on pouring!

Q11. Jesus used His surroundings as He found them without feeling a need to decorate them or alter them substantially. He trusted God to supply the food, and He involved other people in the cleanup process.

Q12. Jesus knew that some of the crowd would try to force a kingship on Him. Their focus on the temporal was something Jesus recognized (verse 26). He offered them something far better—Himself—and yet all they could do was grumble about His claims to divinity. It's hard to believe these people had just experienced one of the most spectacular, undeniable miracles of all time, and yet they still had doubts about whether or not Jesus was from heaven.

Q13. Possible answers:

    a. The miracles took place in two different locations.

    b. The miracle of the feeding of the four thousand is recorded in two gospels that also record the story of the feeding of the five thousand.

    c. Each begins with a different amount of food.

    d. Each records a different amount of leftovers.

    e. A different number of people were present at each miracle.

Q14. The ministry of Jesus was divided into three sections: His work with the Jews, at the end of which He fed the five thousand; His brief visit to the Gentile cities of Tyre, Sidon, and Decapolis, after which He fed the four thousand; and His final visit to Jerusalem, where He hosted the Last Supper.

4 / ATTITUDES IN SERVING: MARTHA'S STORY

Q1. The first time we meet Martha in Scripture, we are impressed with the fact that she so willingly opened her home to the controversial "Prophet" and His disciples. She and her sister Mary were apparently unmarried and were willing to bring upon themselves possible gossip and criticism from their neighbors. We also appreciate Martha for being willing to do the hard physical labor involved in preparing meals for thirteen hungry men. These characteristics remind us of the Shunammite woman.

Q2. We see Martha's weakness not in that she was unwilling to serve but that she let the actual details of the work "get to" her. She had volunteered to provide food and lodging, but she probably did so with the idea that her sister Mary would help her. It wasn't that she didn't want to work—she just didn't want to do *all* the work.

Q3. When we think of Mary sitting at Jesus' feet, we can picture her sitting reverently, listening to what He said as He conversed with her and with His disciples. It is quite possible, though, that she had greeted Jesus as soon as He entered the house and had knelt at His feet to wash them off after the dusty journey. Then as He spoke, she was probably so enrapt in listening that she forgot to get up. We see symbolized in her posture the service, the submissiveness, and the single-minded devotion to Jesus that He encouraged when He told His followers to "seek first the kingdom of God."

Q4. It seems that if Martha had just wanted to get Mary's help in the kitchen, she probably could have gotten her attention quietly. But Martha was feeling so sorry for herself that she bypassed Mary entirely and instead went directly to Jesus. It is obvious from what she said to Jesus that she expected Him to rebuke Mary.

Q5–6. Perhaps Mary with her more sensitive, quiet spirit had sensed that Jesus just needed to talk, and she willingly listened. What He gave her there—words of eternal life—could never be erased from her mind, whereas a few years later Martha probably would be hard pressed to remember the menu she had prepared.

Jesus did not criticize the work that Martha had done to honor Him. But He was saddened to see that instead of giving her a joyful, satisfied feeling, her work had just made her worried and upset. He who promised only light burdens to those who followed Him must have been disappointed that someone had taken upon herself a heavy burden that was unnecessary. We must provide both physical and spiritual nourishment for our guests, but we must do it willingly and cheerfully.

Q7. When each class member responds to this question, try to draw out of her why she feels the way she does.

Q8. Both sisters regarded Jesus as a friend. They also knew of His power and hoped He would help them.

Q9. Verse 5 tells us that Jesus loved Martha.

Q10. We see boldness, unwavering faith in Jesus, knowledge about the last resurrection, and confession of Christ as the Son of God. We also see unselfishness—she went back to the house to get Mary.

Q11. Both Mary and Martha began their conversations with Jesus with the same words, but the more practical Martha went on to express her faith in Jesus, while sensitive Mary was overcome with weeping.

Q12. There are many possible answers, but one must be that He was able to keep His composure when talking with Martha, but He was moved to tears by Mary's tears.

Q13. Perhaps Jesus was thinking of the fact that He himself would be suffering death in just a few days. We know that He loved Mary, Martha, and Lazarus, and He must have been distressed to see them separated. Perhaps Lazarus was the wage-earner for the two women, and they would be reduced to begging without him. Another possible explanation is that He felt frustration against the powers of death and Satan that He had not yet fully conquered.

One Bible translator, Rieu, rendered the phrase, "He was deeply moved in spirit and troubled" as "He gave way to such distress of spirit as made His body tremble." Whatever caused Jesus to break down crying is perhaps not for us to understand. What is important is that by His actions here we can see how deeply He cares for those He loves, and how deeply He is hurt when we are hurting.

Q14. Here we see the same Martha who had expressed unlimited faith in Jesus and His powers worrying about a smell.

Q15. Encourage class members to suggest answers.

Q16. Jesus wanted to thank God for His power in a way that would show non-believers that God had sent Him. Verse 45 tells us that many Jews came to believe in Jesus after Lazarus was raised from the dead.

Q17. Jesus, of course, was the servant here.

Q18. Jesus was the person who was honored.

Q19. The details of the Matthew passage concur in almost every point with the John passage, except that from Matthew we learn that the feast took place in the home of a man named Simon the Leper. The John passage would seem to say that this took place in Lazarus' house until we read it carefully—it simply states that Bethany was where the feast took place, and Bethany was where Lazarus, whom Jesus had raised from the dead, also lived. The leader should also point out that in Luke 7:36–50 we read of an earlier anointing of Jesus in the home of a man named Simon the Pharisee. However except for the coincidental similarity of names of the two Simons and the fact that someone poured perfume on Jesus, the stories of this sinful woman in Luke and the story of Mary's anointing are totally different in content and are in different periods of Jesus' life.

Q20. Here we see Martha doing what she did well—cooking and serving—but this time, apparently, without complaint. And it is beautiful to see her doing so in the home of someone else. Apparently she had learned from her own experiences how draining it was to be hospitable to a crowd, and she was willing to contribute her experience and her hands in doing the labor.

Q21. The disciples were incensed at what they viewed as waste. They thought the money could be spent better on the poor, and Judas probably had in mind that he wouldn't be able to pilfer any of the benefits of this expensive gift. They had a point—some fifteen thousand dollars is a lot of money!

Q22. We are surprised by who didn't speak out—Martha. Whether or not Mary had discussed her plan with her sister ahead of time is not known, but Martha's silence implied that she, too, was pleased with Mary's loving actions.

Q23. Martha must be remembered for her frankness, her ability to "bounce back" without resentment when she was rebuked, her willingness to serve others even when it involved hard work, and also for the fact that she was willing both to recognize fault in her life—and to change!

Q24. Leaders should plan to spend at least ten minutes on this question. Some areas of discussion could include: how to prepare for guests ahead of time, what to look for in guests' behavior that would indicate a need to talk, and the importance of prayer in changing attitudes.

5 / JESUS, THE PERFECT HOST

Q1. The Passover was an annual commemoration of the passing over of the death angel while the Israelites were being held as slaves in Egypt. The Passover meal consisted of an unblemished lamb or kid that was sacrificed in the temple; a part of the lamb along with a money offering was then given to the priests. The animal was then taken home and roasted whole. The house was ceremonially searched for leaven, and bread that was baked without leaven was served to remind the Jews of the haste with which they left Egypt. Bitter herbs, to remind them of the bitterness of their service in Egypt, were served along with a sauce and several cups of wine. Through this celebration the Jews remembered the enduring love and care of the Lord for those who obey Him.

Q2. This feast was very important to the Jews. Even in the twentieth century, Jews faithfully celebrate the Passover each year, always with the prayer that the next year they will be able to eat it in Jerusalem. The modern-day Passover meal does not include the lamb because Deuteronomy 16:2 specifies that it must be killed in the national sanctuary which ceased to exist when Jerusalem was destroyed in A.D. 70.

Jesus knew how important this ritual was to His disciples and He was willing to fill their need for it. He also used the traditional elements of the feast to show them that He was the great sacrifice that the Passover feast had foreshadowed.

Q3. Again we see in Jesus a characteristic of a good host and a good leader: He allowed others the satisfaction of sharing in service.

Q4. Carrying a water pot was considered degrading work for a man in Bible times. No man would be caught dead doing it! It was an unmistakable sign to Peter and John, and we are filled with gratitude for the nameless man who was willing to do "woman's work" to further the Lord's kingdom.

Q5. I personally believe that Jesus had prearranged this signal with a believer in Jerusalem who was perhaps too afraid of pressure from his friends and neighbors to openly serve Christ. But this man did secure lodging for Jesus at a time when accommodations were hard to find.

Q6. This was the last chance Jesus had to meet together with all twelve of His disciples. As the last chapters of John show us, He had much to tell them.

Q7. Jesus possibly thanked God for His disciples, for strength for Himself and for them in the coming days, and for the privilege of serving others.

Q8. Jesus said that the cup was the "new covenant" for which He would shed His blood. Perhaps the passing around of the cup would later remind them of their responsibility to share this covenant with others.

Q9. One possible explanation is that Jesus had complete control over His own body—His life—and would only give it up when the appointed time would come. No one could take it away from Him (John 10:17–18).

Q10. Jesus must have spent several hours telling the disciples His "last minute" instructions. He used the relaxed atmosphere generated by full stomachs and resting, reclining bodies to share with them in a deep, intimate way they would never forget.

Q11. Even with all He must have had on His mind, Jesus still remembered to show His submission to His guests in the most humble way possible. This is also an example of how Jesus took very seriously His duties of making His guests comfortable.

Q12. Jesus was trying to warn them about the way that others would think that His gospel was "turning the world upside down" (Acts 17:6). Their lives would be endangered, but as He would show later that night when Peter cut off the ear of Malchus (John 18:10), Jesus intended that His message be one of healing, not destruction.

Q13. John 6:53–58 tells us that Jesus promised four things to those who would "eat the flesh of the Son of Man and drink his blood." They would:

1. have eternal life.
2. be raised up at the last day.
3. remain in Jesus, and Jesus would remain in them.
4. live because of Him.

Q14. Some suggested areas of emphasis: being a careful listener, assuring them that confidences will be kept just between the two of you, letting them know that your home will be open to them in the future.

Additional exercise:

Divide the class into two groups and select a leader for each group. Have one group read about the Last Supper from Matthew 26:17–30 and have the other group read about the Last Supper from Mark 14:12–25. Instruct the groups to examine how their passages differ from Luke's account. Suggest that the group leaders write down the essential elements of each account as their group members suggest them. Allow about five minutes for this and then reunite the groups and let the two group leaders present what they have found.

6 / HOSPITALITY IN THE EARLY CHURCH

Q1. In A.D. 49 the emperor Claudius (the same as in *I, Claudius*) expelled all Jews from Rome. The great persecutions of Christians that Jesus had predicted had come to pass, and Christians found that they had to depend upon each other more than ever before.

Q2. Verse 3 indicates that they were all tentmakers. We are encouraged to see the couple have in their home someone who might have been a business competitor in a time when their finances must have been very tight after their sudden move from Rome.

Q3. They apparently shared their home with Paul. We do not know from the passage whether or not Priscilla and Aquila were Christians when Paul met them. We only know that they were of the Jewish race.

Q4. If Priscilla and Aquila were not Christians when Paul met them, it must have taken them only a short while to accept the glad message he brought. By the time that Paul left for Syria, Priscilla and Aquila accompanied him as brother and sister in the gospel.

Q5. Verse 26 tells us that they also invited Apollos into their home.

Q6. They were all of Jewish origin; Priscilla and Aquila undoubtedly remembered how someone had taken the time and shown them love and taught them the way of Christ.

Q7. The teachings of all the Old Testament prophets urged the people to repent—to change their hearts and their actions. And if Apollos knew of Jesus' life, he must have known that He fit exactly the Messianic prophecies of the Old Testament. In fact, the gospel of Matthew, which was written to Jews, would have been a great tool for teaching someone like Apollos because Matthew was very careful to list at least sixteen different instances where the actions of Jesus "fulfilled what was spoken by the prophet." However we are not sure when Matthew wrote, and this may not have been available to Apollos.

Q8. Note how kindly Priscilla and Aquila refrained from

publicly criticizing Apollos, choosing instead to use the friendly atmosphere of their home to teach him.

Q9. Diane and Robert Bloem in their leader's manual for *A Woman's Workshop On Bible Marriages* point out the following:

• Paul's teaching of submission by wives agrees with Peter's teaching in 1 Peter 3:1–2.

• Teaching is a part of prophesying. The gift of prophecy was given to men and women (Acts 2:16–18; 1 Corinthians 12:7–11). This is further evidenced by the mention of several prophetesses: Miriam (Exodus 15:20); Deborah (Judges 4:4); Huldah (2 Kings 22:14); Anna (Luke 2:36); and the four daughters of Philip (Acts 21:9).

• Priscilla taught with her husband.

• Priscilla did not take away authority from her husband or from Apollos.

• Priscilla did this teaching in her own home.

Priscilla and Aquila were Paul's personal pupils and were closely involved with him in his teaching and the practice of his teachings. They would have understood the intent of his words. Thus if this had been a violation, they would have realized it and conformed to the teaching.

Q10. Apollos must have been impressed with their openness and kindness. These qualities always soften the heart of someone who is willing to learn.

Q11. Encourage class members to share some teachings that might have helped Apollos. Don't let the class get too far astray on teaching methods, though.

Q12. They encouraged him and wrote letters of introduction to the disciples in Achaia.

Q13. Although Paul might not have had personal contact with the Achaian Jews that Apollos taught, Paul was the one who had taught Priscilla and Aquila who in turn taught Apollos.

Q14. Apollos possessed the ability to debate and prove from Scripture that Jesus was the Christ. He used this ability to refute the Jews of Achaia in public debate.

Q15. Barclay in his commentary on 1 Corinthians noted that "... wherever Priscilla and Aquila went, their home became a church."

Q16. This question and the one after it are discussion questions for which there are no firm answers. Encourage class members to contribute. Example: "Perhaps Priscilla was the motivating force in the couple's spiritual life."

Q17. Possible answers:

    a. Paul was a dangerous person to be around because he was always in trouble with the law.

    b. The couple probably had suffered financial loss in their move and might not have had a lot to share.

    c. Perhaps their new home was not large enough or as fancy as they would have liked.

7 / HOSPITALITY, THE HEALER

Q1. When we first see the jailer, we know he must have realized how Paul and Silas had been punished. Perhaps he had even witnessed the beatings. He knew how important these prisoners were, and he took pains to put them into the innermost cell and to further confine them in stocks that would prevent them from even dressing each other's wounds.

Q2. Perhaps the jailer was hardened to such scenes of human suffering; at any rate, he obeyed his superiors implicitly—either out of duty or perhaps fear.

Q3. Emphasize that there was no such thing as prisoners' rights in those days. Keep this part of the discussion brief, but remind class members that there were no toilets, disease was rampant, torture of prisoners was commonplace, and many died of starvation or malnutrition. There were rats, other vermin, and many other factors that caused people of the day to consider a prisoner to be dead the moment he entered prison because his chances were so slim of returning to his home.

Q4. Paul and Silas began praying and singing hymns to God which aroused the attention of the other prisoners.

Q5. Many jailers in ancient times were killed if they allowed a prisoner to escape. Perhaps it was disorientation caused by the earthquake or the calming, encouraging singing of Paul and Silas or even fear that caused the other prisoners not to escape.

Q6. Perhaps he was afraid, but more likely he realized that the earthquake was a sign of the divine power of God, and he wanted to ally himself with this Power not oppose it.

Q7. He had seen their good cheer in suffering and their consideration of his feelings in letting him know all the prisoners were there so he wouldn't kill himself.

Q8. He bound up their wounds before asking them to baptize him. Then he fed them.

Q9. Allow about three minutes each for this discussion question. Draw out answers from quieter group members.

Q10. The jailer had stood by and watched the two men be stripped and severely beaten, and then he had himself put them into cruelly confining stocks. Choose three class members and have them do an impromptu dialogue of what they think the conversation must have been as the jailer washed the wounds of Paul and Silas.

The jailer was showing his trust of his prisoners to take them into his home. He was also demonstrating his repentance by offering them hospitality. The most amazing thing seen in this section, though, is the loving acceptance that Paul and Silas showed toward the jailer.

Q11. The leader should be ready with a specific example from her own life that will "spark" other answers.

Q12. Emphasize here that offering hospitality can be the first step in mending a relationship, and it will soften the heart of the person who has wronged you when they see that you are not only willing to sacrifice to fill their physical needs but that you are also willing to share a part of yourself by opening your home to them.

8 / EXCUSES, EXCUSES

Excuse #1

The discussion leader should take her cue from the personality of her group to decide how much time and what emphasis to put on each of the four excuses. A group made up of only homemakers, for instance, would not want to spend a lot of time discussing how working makes you too tired to be a good hostess. Instead, the leader could focus on the fatigue we all occasionally feel.

Q1. Jesus' promise has several parts: an invitation ("Come to me"), an understanding statement of our condition ("you . . . are weary and burdened"), a responsibility ("take my yoke . . . and learn of me"), a guarantee ("I will give you rest . . . you shall find rest"), and a reassurance ("my yoke is easy and my burden is light"). We often think of the burden that we hand over to Jesus as being our sin, from which He releases us; but we limit the power of this great promise if we don't hand over to Him *anything* that prevents us from functioning at our full potential.

Q2. Most of our burdens are self-imposed, even though we may say we are doing things for our families or for our employers or even for our churches. But the important thing to remember is that it doesn't matter where a burden comes from—it only matters whether we struggle along under it alone or exchange it for Jesus' lightweight yoke. In terms of being hospitable when we think it might make us more tired, the first step might be asking the Lord to help us. As soon as we begin to feel pressure or fatigue, if we will immediately go to Him, He will take those burdens and trade them for a feeling of peaceful rest.

Q3. One pracitcal way to take pressure off yourself is to ask guests to bring a dish when they come. One couple I know has had amazing success at keeping a consistently high attendance at their weekly, in-home, evangelistic Bible study. Their secret? They always ask non-Christians to bring their favorite dessert. Besides having a chance to show off a favorite treat, the non-Christians are also assured that their presence is being counted on. Other suggestions for the busy working woman could include: co-hosting guests with another working woman, first in your home and then in hers (cuts the work in half and doubles the fun); having the teenagers from your church over (they won't care if your house is clean or not as long as there are lots of soft drinks, chips, dips, and games); or calling a nearby rest home to see if there is an ambulatory patient there who would benefit from a visit in your home or dinner at a restaurant.

Excuse #2

Q1. A wife's first responsibility is to cultivate a gentle and quiet spirit that is demonstrated in her submission to her husband. This doesn't mean she should become a doormat; but she should seek to respect her husband's wishes and try to please him. If having guests angers her husband, she should find other avenues of Christian service.

Q2. The typical non-Christian husband doesn't care if his wife has guests over during the day as long as his dinner is prepared and the house is in order when he comes home. Daytime, in fact, is an ideal time to have elderly people in your home because many older people cannot drive at night.

Q3. It is important to emphasize that just because a woman with an unbelieving husband cannot "use" her home in the same manner as a woman with a Christian husband, this does not mean she cannot serve others with her home's resources as long as she does not antagonize her husband. Also, many non-Christian husbands who do not encourage their wives to invite adults into their homes will not object to their children inviting their young friends. It has always been my experience that God will provide an opportunity for service if we truly wish to serve.

Excuse #3

Q1. God promises that if we will be generous with whatever we have, not only will He supply our own needs but He will give us "extra" so that we can "be generous on every occasion" (verse 11). This is like having a savings account that earns interest on the interest that the bank gave you for putting your money in their bank in the first place. On both the financial and spiritual levels the same principle applies: Unless you withdraw, you can't lose!

Q2. We must remember that the primary contact most non-Christians have with God is what they see of Him reflected in His followers. If they see us loving and generous, they conclude that He must be the same. But, as Romans 2:23–24 shows us, the opposite is equally true.

Q3. Some possible answers could include: all grace will abound to you (verse 8), you will abound in every good work (verse 8), the harvest of your righteousness will be increased (verse 10), you will be made rich in every way (verse 11), others will pray for you (verse 14).

Q4. One obvious way to have people in your home for a meal is to host a pot-luck or covered-dish dinner. Many women in our congregation have done this on a regular basis, rotating homes and inviting new Christians to come to their homes and bring a salad of some sort. The hostess supplies the drinks. Another way a young and financially struggling couple I know offers hospitality by inviting friends over in the evenings for popcorn and iced tea and games like charades. Everyone has a ball!

Excuse #4

Q1. James would probably say that all the good intentions in the world that are not translated into action are useless because they can't be perceived by others. In fact, good thoughts without follow-up action could even be seen as hypocrisy.

Q2. Verses 15 and 16 mention two specific needs—food and clothing—that are ideally met by hospitality. Other needs might include shelter, refuge (as in the case of a battered wife), spiritual encouragement, training (as in the case of a new mother), Bible instruction, and of course fellowship and love.

The best way to fill each guest's needs is to try to take a moment before she arrives to ask yourself, "What is it that I can give that this guest needs today?" Then mentally note something you could do to fill that need.

Q3. You might offer to help that shy sister prepare for her guests. If you know her guests very well, you could tell her their interests so she could be prepared to set them at ease by asking some good "discussion-starter" questions. Assure your friend that you will pray for her, too.

9 / THE BEST HOSPITALITY

Q1. Both passages emphasize the fact that there will be final "accounting" of our deeds.

Q2. This was Jesus' final parable. Like a last will and testament, it must have conveyed many feelings that He wanted to make sure that the disciples remembered and understood.

Q3. Jesus compares the righteous to sheep and goats, when in actuality He is referring to people. But the parable is set in a definite future time period, thus showing that it is telling about something that will really happen.

Q4. Verse 34 says the kingdom has been prepared for us "since the creation of the world."

Q5. Other than going to a prison to visit, all the services could be provided in your home. In the case of a prisoner, hospitality could be offered while he or she might be on parole.

Q6. They are obviously surprised.

Q7. Apparently they had served others with no thought of future reward, but they had enjoyed the satisfaction that the service itself provided.

Q8. Perhaps this passage is saying that the people that our pride causes us to pass over when we're making out guest lists are precisely the people we should actively try to have in our homes. They may be "least" to us but greatest in God's estimation.

Q9. It is a characteristic of our loving God that He never intended hell for people but for the rebellious angels and their reprobate leader, Satan. It is only by willful disobedience such as this that a person can force his or her way into hell.

Q10. All of these things happened to Jesus just a few days later, in the hours before His death.

Q11–12. The unrighteous were surprised, too, but sought to excuse their negligence by saying they didn't realize the consequences of their action. That is true—when we realize that we are serving Christ when we serve others, we do act differently.

Q13. It is by reading the Bible, attending church, and prayer that God communicates with us the need for serving others.

Q14. If the group feels "goatish," discuss some concrete avenues of change, such as getting involved in a prison ministry.

Q15. This verse encourages us by showing us that Jesus is willing to come into our hearts if we just open the door to Him. The delightful prospect of sharing the hospitality of our heart to such a considerate, loving guest is one of the most wonderful promises in Scripture.

SUGGESTED READING FOR FURTHER STUDY

Bloem, Diane Brummel and Robert C. *A Woman's Workshop On Bible Marriages.* Grand Rapids, Michigan: The Zondervan Corporation, 1980.

Deen, Edith. *Family Living in the Bible.* New York: Harper & Row Publs., Inc., 1963.

Hall, Vivian Anderson, *Be My Guest.* Chicago: Moody Press, 1979.

LeFever, Marlene. *Creative Hospitality.* Wheaton, Illinois: Tyndale House Publishers, Inc., 1980.

Mains, Karen Burton. *Open Heart, Open Home.* Elgin, Illinois: David C. Cook Publishing Co., 1977.

Simpson, Peggy. *Hospitality in the Spirit of Love.* Abilene, Texas: Quality Publications, 1980.